DEDICATION

This book, "Perform Like A Champion Every Time You Speak" is dedicated to everyone, aspiring to share their message with the world. The world needs great leaders that are willing to standout and stand up for what they believe in. Your voice matters and you must let it be heard. Positivity is craved and greatly needed in today's society. Share your knowledge freely, to elevate, inspire and empower others around you. In love & light always!!!

CONTENTS

ACKNOWLEDGMENTS i

FOREWORD ii

INTRODUCTION 1

CHAPTER 1: INTERESTING
Do You Know Who You Are? 16

CHAPTER 2: MOVEMENT
The Hidden Code Of Natural Presenters 28

    Archetypes 30

    The Warrior Gesture 31

    The Lover Gesture 34

    The Sage Gesture 37

    The Jester Gesture 40

    The Sovereign Gesture 43

    The Neutral Gesture 44

CHAPTER 3: PRESENCE
Show Up 100% Every Time You Speak 47

CHAPTER 4: AWARENESS
How to Shift the Mood of Your Audience 60

PERFORM LIKE A CHAMPION EVERY TIME YOU SPEAK

HOW TO HAVE OUTSTANDING PRESENTATION SKILLS

TOSIN OGUNNUSI

Disclaimer

This book is designed to provide information and motivation to our readers. It is sold with the understanding that the author and publisher are not engaged to render any type of psychological, legal, or any other kind of professional advice. The content is the sole expression and opinion of its author. Neither the publisher nor the individual author(s) shall be liable for any physical, psychological, emotional, financial, or commercial damages, including, but not limited to, special, incidental, consequential or other damages. Our views and rights are the same: You are responsible for your own choices, actions, and results.

The content of the book is solely written by the author.

DVG STAR Publishing are not liable for the content of the book.

Published by DVG STAR PUBLISHING

www.dvgstar.com

email us at info@dvgstar.com

NO PART OF THIS WORK MAY BE REPRODUCED OR STORED IN AN INFORMATIONAL RETRIEVAL SYSTEM, WITHOUT THE EXPRESS PERMISSION OF THE PUBLISHER IN WRITING.

Copyright © 2019 Tosin Ogunnusi

All rights reserved.

ISBN: 1-912547-38-4
ISBN-13: 978-1-912547-38-8

CHAPTER 5: CONNECTION
The Secret To Making Your Audience Feel Special 66

CHAPTER 6: TONALITY
How Do You Engage Your Audience with Your Voice? 72

CHAPTER 7: PUTTING IT ALTOGETHER 79

TOSIN OGUNNUSI'S SPEAKING JOURNEY 88

TESTIMONIALS 101

ACKNOWLEDGMENTS

A huge thank you to all my mentors because without them I wouldn't be where I am today. I couldn't do what I do without my wife (Anna Ogunnusi). Thank you sweetness for your continued belief in me and your selfless support. In love & light always!

FOREWORD

Learning to public speak is one of the best things I have ever done, and I would certainly say, it has opened more opportunities for me and my businesses than ANYTHING else I have ever learned or mastered.

It really still surprises me, that still to this day it is one of the most feared skills, and yet one of the most effective ways to move people and build an empire or push your message out.

Maybe this is because, there is something unique still, about the act of standing on a stage, that makes people look up and listen to you and your message, its powerful.

In this modern day world, this also now transcribes to making a video, a podcast or a Facebook live too, which all seem to have the same authority building effect, that presenting does, and thankfully many of the same skillsets are shared between all of these activities.

I learned to speak back in 2009, when social media was still new, and I learnt by speaking at landlord networking events all around the UK, I took every gig I could get my hands on, any stage anywhere, to get used to speaking in front of a live audience, and after 18 months, all the fear had gone completely, but I was still a rough diamond.

I had never learned how to structure a talk, my stance, tone and audience engagement was a bit rough, I needed work.

I embarked on a coaching programme for professional speakers, and that's where I met Tosin, and it all started to "click" I could see where I had been going wrong, I had been literally rocking up and waffling!

When I learnt the skills Tosin teaches in this book, I could FEEL the change of state in the audience, with not what I was saying but

HOW I was saying it, the change was immense. I connected with more of the audience, they understood and more importantly FELT understood more as a result.

The changes are subtle but 100 times more powerful, than you can ever imagine.

Since learning to speak on stage, I have been asked to speak alongside some of the biggest names in the industry, multiple large scale conferences, and hundreds of smaller summits and seminars, not to mention running hundreds of my own events in the meantime too, plus I have been able to reach 10's of millions online, with video and Facebook Live's.

It's been an amazing 9 years since learning to speak "properly" my business has multiplied many times, my reach has exploded, I have started a movement "Agent Rainmaker" and I hope to change an industry (my industry) for the better as a result of this skill.

But what's really powerful is that this has bought our community together (whereas before there was no way to connect) we have a shared vision, and greater purpose, and lives are being changed as a result.

Speaking is for me the number one skill, and as a coach Tosin is world class, Tosin coaches my Agent Rainmaker speakers for my annual conference every year, and in just a few sessions he somehow manages to take them from standing, shivering in fear to being confident, stage commanding experts. It's amazing what he does, and every year my Agent Rainmaker LIVE event is a testament to him and what he teaches here in this book.

My advice? Read it, consume it, practice it and take control of your message, start a movement, become the voice of your community and change lives… then you can truly say you stood for something and made a difference.

Sally Lawson PPARLA, Founder of Agent Rainmaker

INTRODUCTION

It is said that most people are afraid of speaking in public. Doesn't that make you wonder why that is the case?

The reason for that is, when you really think about it, don't we all speak in public all the time?

You do, don't you? I mean, everyone you know also speaks in public. Granted, it might not be in front of a large audience, but you still speak in public most of the time: In the pub, supermarket and at events with your friends, strangers or loved ones, don't you?

The only reason why you are afraid to do the same in front of a small group or large group is very simple: you think that when you present or speak in front of an audience, you ought to behave and act in a different way to how you are when having a conversation with your mates down the pub.

This is a fundamental flaw most people have when they are presenting and speaking in public.

This book is titled "Perform Like A Champion Every Time You Speak," and it is the first book in our "F1 Speaker System Series." It is written specifically to help you overcome this flaw.

It provides you with an easy, step-by-step guide to implement so that you can perform like a champion every time you speak. Its sole purpose is to answer the question, "How do you acquire outstanding presentation skills?"

In this book, you are about to learn a very unique skill set that is in high demand. Once you've mastered it, it can make your stock value go up, position you as an expert in your industry, and more importantly, you become a key person of influence.

What am I talking about? I'm talking about the skill of becoming a professional public speaker. The skill of ***"Speaking and Presenting with Impact."***

Whether you are presenting to a large audience, on a webinar, live on camera, one-to-one, or in a small boardroom meeting, it doesn't matter. This skill is invaluable.

You will learn and pick up these skills through our unique "Formula 1 Speaker System Series."

The Formula 1 Speaker System is designed to take you from a go-kart speaker to a Formula 1 speaker in just a matter of weeks and months… guaranteed!

So, permit me to share with you what the "F1 Speaker System Series" has in store for you. There are three fundamental questions that the "F1 Speaker System Series" actually answers.

Series 1 (Perform Like A Champion Every Time You Speak) is all about your delivery and performance. As a speaker and presenter you need to ultimately have outstanding presentation skills in order for you to deliver your message with real impact, gusto and conviction.

You see, you may have a great message to share, but if you share it with no presence, no energy, and no real impact, then people won't believe you. Your message will fall flat and crucially people won't buy into your message, which means they won't act on your message, and in some instances that could be very costly for you, your business (if you have one) or the organisation you work for.

What you are actually learning here is the answer to the fundamental question that most people who are afraid of public speaking would ask:

*"How do you **acquire outstanding** presentation skills?"*

That's the first question.

Series 2 (Inform Like A Champion Every Time You Speak) is all about how you share your know-how by creating a Unique Identity Framework, or a Solution Framework if you like. In this book you will learn tactics and strategies for putting your knowledge into a cohesive system that anyone can learn from, which would mean you can now leverage your effort by teaching others how to deliver what you deliver, and start delivering one-to-many instead of just one-to-one.

What will this do for you or your business? It will position you as an expert in your industry, which now means you can start to charge expert fees. So, creating this solution framework is what is known as your IP (Intellectual Property). It can now become the basis of your book, your video program, online program, or your 1, 2, 3, or 4-day training course. Simply put, it's your ticket to printing your own money. As my good friend Daniel Priestley wrote in his ground-breaking book Entrepreneur Revolution, "Income follows assets!" So, you have to start creating assets and your "Unique Identity Framework" is your asset (Information Base Asset).

What you are actually learning here is the answer to another fundamental question that most people who are afraid of public speaking would ask:

*"How do you **structure** your presentation?"*

Have you ever had to do a presentation, and you really didn't know where to begin?

If you've ever experienced this in the past then do yourself a favour and get the book "Inform Like A Champion Every Time You Speak," which is our second book in our "F1 Speaker System Series."

This second book will show you, step-by step, how to extract your knowledge or know-how and package it in a logical and systematic way so that others can learn directly from you and benefit from your expertise.

Series 3 (Engage & Entertain Like A Champion Every Time You Speak): If you truly want to connect with your audience and make them feel significant and special, then this third book is a must.

Here you will be exposed to tried, tested and proven strategies that have stood the test of time. You will learn practical tips and tools that you can implement straight away into your next presentation or speaking engagement.

What you are actually learning here is the answer to the final fundamental question that most people who are afraid of public speaking would ask:

*"How do you **engage and entertain** your audience?"*

I'm sure you will agree that it is truly important not just to give information but to also transform your audience at the same time? If you agree then the question is how do you do it? How do you do it so that your audience gets your message at a deeper level and, more importantly, they act upon your message? That is what we're talking about here.

So, there you have it, the "F1 Speaker System Series 1, 2 and 3".

So, within these 3 books you are going to be getting answers to the three main fundamental questions:

1. **"How do you acquire great presentation skills?"**

2. **"How do you structure your talk?"**

3. **"How do you engage and entertain your audience?"**

The business owners, coaches, consultants and students who attend our 3-day Speaking & Presenting with I.M.P.A.C.T. live training program learn about the "F1 Speaker System," which contains 6 core modules. These 6 core modules will completely answer the questions above.

Below is a diagram of our F1 Speaker System depicting these 6 core modules:

F1 SPEAKER SYSTEM

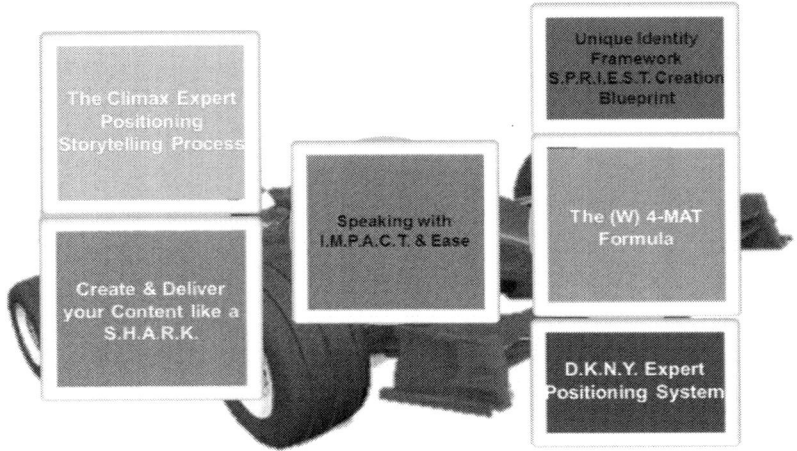

Let's begin in this book, "Perform Like A Champion Every Time You Speak."

Here we look at the first question: "How do you acquire great presentation skills?"

The module to answer this question is called, "Speaking with I.M.P.A.C.T. and Ease."

I.M.P.A.C.T. is an acronym. There are six core skills that you need to master to truly deliver your talk, your presentation, your webinar, your online video, whatever it may be for you, with real impact. Once you've acquired these six core skills and mastered them by implementing them into your speaking engagements, then you can guarantee you will no longer be a boring speaker like every other rookie speaker out there. You'll be engaging, you'll be commanding, people will believe in your message, and you'll speak with a lot more belief and conviction in your voice. That is what this will do for you.

To answer the question of how to structure your talk, we have 3 modules that you need to look at. The first module is what I call The Unique Identity Framework – the S.P.R.I.E.S.T. Creation Blueprint.

S.P.R.I.E.S.T. is an acronym that really stands for being active and agile, meaning you need to have a unique solution for the problem that you are solving for your clients. This is how we do that, through having a unique identity framework that allows you to be able to freely express yourself while you speak.

You'll find that when you do this, you will no longer require notes when you present.

Consider this for a moment - Can you imagine what it would feel like to deliver your entire presentation without having to refer to your notes ever again?

When I use PowerPoint, I only have frameworks. These frameworks allow me to truly express myself when I speak, and you'll be doing exactly the same thing. No longer will you have the need to use notes when you present and no longer will you need to know your content word for word, because ultimately that's just a long-winded approach that doesn't really work long-term.

No matter how hard you prepare or memorise your content, if you analyse it closely, you will find that you didn't perform it word for word. There are most certainly words that you missed or simply replaced unconsciously, guaranteed.

Most speakers write out the entire script of their presentation, and then they go about memorising it word for word. That doesn't work. It doesn't matter how much you memorise that stuff; when you stand on a stage, or just in front of a group of people to present, you're bound to forget something as you are presenting to your audience. You are more likely to appear wooden because what you're doing is trying to remember what you've written down in your head consciously. That doesn't allow you to focus on your audience and fully express yourself whilst you are presenting.

If you look at sports personalities, athletes, and all those kinds of people, when they're playing golf for example, when they're in the game, they're in the game. Everything's unconscious, because you can't consciously think about the game while you're playing the game. It doesn't really work. That is a flawed way of doing things. If you're doing this, stop it because you don't need to do that.

What you need to do instead is to create a unique identity framework that will allow you the freedom of expression, so that you can deliver your message with real I.M.P.A.C.T.

The second module within structuring your talk is what I call "Knowing Your Audience -The W-Format Formula."

There are four 'W's, hence the W-Format Formula.

There are four critical things here that you need to understand in terms of the makeup of the people in your audience.

The W-Format Formula shows you how to motivate your audience because every single one of them is motivated very differently. You'll learn core skills around how to craft your message to cater to these four types of people within your audience.

Here's the thing: When five or more people are gathered together, you're guaranteed to have these four elements within that small group. Therefore, if you're speaking to thirty, forty, fifty, sixty, a hundred people, a thousand people, it doesn't matter the number. There are four types of people within your audience and you need to craft your presentation in a way that really engages each and every one of them. Otherwise, you'll be losing some of your audience.

Most speakers don't even understand this, but when you get this and you apply this in your presentation skills, oh my! No longer will yours be a boring presentation. You'll find that you're engaging sixty, seventy, eighty or even ninety percent of your audiences.

That is the key here: You're getting more people to buy into your message at the end of the day, which is the reason why we're doing it, right?

Ultimately, what everyone who speaks is looking for is to create change. Would you agree with that? Because whatever your solution is to a problem, it must provide a change for the client or the customer. That is, it must solve a problem for them or get them from where there are to where they want to go, and in the end that's why we are all in business. We're in the business of **"CHANGE!"**

The final module here, around structuring your talk, all has to do with your first, ten, fifteen or twenty minutes, when you get on stage or begin any presentation. The real key is how do you start? How do you really begin? How do you really impact your audience? You get this wrong, and everything else is just boring. You get this right? Oh my! You'll have people running to the back of the room wanting to do business with you. You'll have people really knowing, liking, and trusting you and really wanting to come along the journey with you. Get this wrong and there'll be no call to action from your message. It will just fall on deaf ears.

I call this module the "D.K.N.Y. Expert Positioning System." There are four things you need to position right at the beginning of your presentation. When you position these four things, then people are ready and willing to listen to your message.

Finally, before I conclude, I almost forgot. To answer the question *"How do you engage and entertain your audience?"* I have created 2 modules for you around that.

The first one is what I call the "Climax Expert Positioning Storytelling Process."

This module uses basic concepts that Hollywood directors use to create blockbuster Hollywood movies that literally have you on the edge of your seat.

Would you agree that when you sit down and you're engaged and engrossed in a movie for an hour, an hour and twenty minutes, ninety minutes, two hours, three hour movie, that the movie engages all of your senses? That is because there are certain things within the movie that the director has put in place to make sure that they get your full attention, which in turn keeps you glued to your chair watching the movie. In some cases you refuse to take a toilet break just in case you miss something, don't you?

We must do the same thing as presenters and speakers, because here's the truth: You are not just presenters and speakers, you're entertainers as well.

So you need to also add some of these key elements of movie making into your storytelling process. You'll agree that every great professional speaker out there, every great orator out there today that you like and admire, are all great storytellers by and large.

Looking back into history, you would find that even Jesus Christ and our forefathers were great storytellers.

I actually remember back in Africa, all the children would sit by the campfire and the elders would come and tell us stories about what happened in their lives and throughout history. They would talk about wars, all that stuff. They'd sit down and tell us stories, and those stories were engaging. They were intriguing and gripping at the same time.

This is how you need to be able to tell great stories. You might want to write this down. This is crucial and this is important. If you want to influence people, and you want to make an impact with your message, then learn to master the art of storytelling, because content tells and stories sell.

"Storytelling is selling, and selling is storytelling."

Get that right, and ultimately your message will be absolutely dynamite.

Finally, to engage your audience, we also have what I call "Creating and Delivering Your Content Like a S.H.A.R.K."

S.H.A.R.K. is an acronym. Literally, there are five key steps that you need to learn to allow you to expand on your message.

For Instance, when you have your Unique Identity Framework, or your solution framework, you will have points on it like I have points here (S.H.A.R.K.). Then the question is, how do you develop/create content for each individual point? It's not just bullet points and revealing what the S or H or A or R or K stands for, and then you're done. It's a lot more than that.

The presentation for each point can be ten minutes, fifteen minutes, twenty minutes or even half an hour in some cases. So, the question we are seeking to answer here is, *"How do you elaborate on your point and how do you deliver it with real I.M.P.A.C.T.?"*

This is exactly what you will gain by implementing the S.H.A.R.K. module.

Once you have these five key steps mastered, I'm telling you right now, you'll never run out of things to say. You'll never worry about creating content. You can just do it at will. Someone can say, *"Hey, do you want to talk about change?"* You say, *"Change, hold on a minute. Let me run it through the S.H.A.R.K. model."* And in just a few minutes you are ready to deliver on the topic of change with real IMPACT! Just like magic. It's a formula, if you like.

Okay. There you have it. That's the overview of the Formula 1 Speaker System.

Just to recap, the Formula 1 Speaker System will answer three core major issues that affect people out there who want to present or speak in public. Other professionals, business owners, coaches and consultants also experience some of these challenges, if not all.

1. **How do you acquire great presentation skills?**
2. **How do you structure your presentation?**
3. **How do you engage and entertain your audience?**

So, to answer these questions, you will be learning about the F1 Speaker System where I will take you step-by-step through the book series, explaining in detail the six core skills or six core modules, if you like:

1. Speaking with I.M.P.A.C.T. & Ease.

2. The Unique Identity Framework - S.P.R.I.E.S.T. Creation Blueprint.

3. Know Your Audience - The W-Format Formula.

4. The D.K.N.Y. Expert Positioning System.

5. The Climax Expert Positioning Storytelling Process

6. Creating and Delivering Content Like a S.H.A.R.K.

If you are like me and you like to learn by watching and doing and not just by reading, then you can visit our website: www.mpowerment.co.uk/training-programmes and go ahead and purchase our Online Speaker Training. There are videos explaining, demonstrating and outlining the entire F1 Speaker System.

It's then up to you to start implementing the strategies into your presentation skills as you get out there to speak and present with real I.M.P.A.C.T.

So, let's get started! This book is all about answering the question,

"How do you acquire outstanding presentation skills?"

"How do you go out there and perform like a champion every time you speak?"

"How do you go from a go-cart speaker into a Formula 1 speaker in a matter weeks and months, not years?"

That's what we're going to be covering in this unique, easy to read and implement book.

You can have a great script or a great presentation or a great talk, speech, etc. But, if you can't deliver it with real gusto, conviction, and impact then it will fall flat…meaning your message won't be believable and people won't take you seriously. More importantly, they won't act upon your message.

If you want people to see you as authentic, unique, somebody who knows what they're talking about, measured, poised, balanced, somebody who people are going to get to know, like, and trust and ultimately do business with and take action on your message, then you have to master the skills in this book.

First of all, what is the, "Speaking With I.M.P.A.C.T and Ease Model?"

Now, speaking with I.M.P.A.C.T and Ease is absolutely magical. There are 6 things here that you need to master in order for you to deliver your message with real impact.

This is a model that will allow you to present any material or topic with ease and impact. It does exactly what it says on the tin.

Let's look at the 6 things individually and then go through them in detail so that you really understand what to do in order to experience them in your own presentations:

1. **Interesting:**
   Do you know who you are?

2. **Movement:**
   The hidden code for natural presenters

3. **Presence:**
   Show up 100% every time you speak

4. **Awareness:**
   How to shift the mood of your audience

5. **Connection:**
   The secret to making your audience feel special

6. **Tonality:**
   How do you engage your audience with your voice?

CHAPTER 1
INTERESTING
Do You Know Who You Are?

What's the very first thing you need to know? Well, I just gave it away there by asking the question above. Do you know who you are? What does that mean? Well that means do you know yourself?

What I'm talking about here is that the "I" in (I.M.P.A.C.T.) is Interesting. Would you say that you're an interesting character? Yes or no? Absolutely! Would you say I'm an interesting character too? You bet I am, 100%! You see, you and I and everybody else we're very different from each other. And that's the key, because you have your own nuances, idiosyncrasies, mannerisms, characteristics, attributes, your own energy signature and so on and so forth. There are no two people on planet Earth that are alike; even identical twins are interestingly different.

Now, hear me very clearly: It is this interesting part of you that other people really want to connect with. The bottom-line is, people are buying into you, or not, as the case may be. That is why you have to stand out and be yourself. You have to be interesting and different. What I'm talking about here is about you being yourself and not trying to be somebody else. Therefore, you are authentic, you are open, you are trustworthy and you are transparent, because in the information age that we live in, and the social media era we're living in now, if you're not any of those things, you'll be found out very easily. Many people say one thing, and then they do something else instead. Well you can't afford to do that here. In this industry you'll be found out very quickly.

You have to be yourself. I mean if you don't know something, then admit openly that you don't know. If you're learning, you're learning.

The question I want to ask you is, if there were three words to describe you as a person, what would those three words be? What would somebody else say about you?

My spiritual mentor once asked me a very interesting question, and I'm going to pose the same question to you. He asked me, *"Tosin, if you were to die tomorrow, what would people say about you?"*

Food for thought, right?

So, if you were to die tomorrow, what do you think the people around you would say about you? What are you about? What drives you?

Think about it! It's ultimately when you know what you're about, when you know who you are. It's your brand. It's not just when you're up on stage you're one person and when you're off stage you're somebody else, which most professional speakers are like.

You want to be different, so that who you are on stage is who you are off stage. Period!!!

You don't want there to be any difference between who you are on stage and off stage, because you're the brand and people buy into you. This is crucial. What are you about, what do you stand for? Who are you? Find those things out, because once you know who you are and what you're about, then you can be you. The question is, in every single scenario are you being yourself? Are you being you with your loved ones? Are you being you with your spouse? Are you being you with your children? Are you being you around your clients and your customers? Are you being you around your business partners?

Interesting, isn't it? Because anything less than being you is not being authentic.

Ultimately we're talking about being interesting. We're talking about authentic living.

One of the biggest mistake that people make, which prevents them from being themselves, is they compare themselves to other people. Listen to me closely: That is a dumb game, as my mentor would say. Actually, it's not a dumb game, it's a stupid game, and if you're doing it, stop it. How can you compare your number one with somebody else's number 20 or 200? You can't!

You see, we're all essentially the same. As in if I cut my hand, red blood will come out, and if you cut yours, red blood comes out too, not green blood. We share the same nervous system, regardless of our colour, sex, religion or country of origin. We're all connected, as my mentor would say; we're a spiritual being, having a human experience. Regardless of what your culture is and where you're from, it doesn't matter, and I identify with that really well. It allows no judgment. You realise that we are essentially the same, but what makes you stand out, what makes you unique?

I believe what makes you stand out and unique are your little characteristics, your mannerisms, your attitude, your behaviours and your results. That's what makes you special from the rest.

Often people see me as having child-like characteristics because I like to have fun. I like to engage with children and be around children and those who are fun to be around.

With my children I'm the biggest child of the lot, because that's what I'm about. I like to have a bit of fun. I'm not talking about being a child but having child-like characteristics. Most adults have forgotten what that feels like to have a child-like, playful attitude. Do you remember what it felt like to be a child?

So, what I'm asking you to do is be interesting, be you, and that's what we're talking about here. If you're not being you and you're comparing yourself to somebody else, then you're doing yourself a big injustice, because that's not a like for like comparison, is it?

Here's what you need to be measuring yourself by: Are you better than you were yesterday? Are you better than you were last week? Are you better than you were last month? Are you better than you were last year? Are you better than you were 5 years ago? Are you better than you were 10 years ago?

If you are, then congratulations and pat yourself on the back, because you're doing something different. You are growing and improving. Continue to improve yourself, whether you're learning a new language or you're learning a new skill, trying to do something new, a new sport, a new activity. All of those things are great because you're improving yourself in some shape or form, and you're gaining valuable skills in the process of doing so.

It's not really about trying to be better than everybody else and comparing yourself to somebody else or measuring yourself against somebody else, no. Ultimately, being yourself is about living a happy life, and a happy life is different for everybody. What makes you happy might be completely different from what makes me happy. Find out what that is for you.

When speaking, it is absolutely crucial that you know who you are, and that you are comfortable within your own skin. You see, speaking is an unconscious process, but people try to make it too conscious, and perhaps you're doing the same, or thinking too much.

The goal for you is to be out there with your audience sharing your message, and you do this by focusing on the value that you bring to the table.

Now most rookie speakers are too busy being in their own heads by focusing on themselves. I call this being sell…fish. When you're selling fish in the market, you stink, because fish smell. What you need to be doing instead is you need to be selfless and stop worrying about what people think of you.

You know what, I've got news for you: You're not important in that process. People don't really care what you look like. People don't really care what you're doing. What people care about is the message that you're about to deliver to them, as in, the value you bring to the table. So, stop worrying about how you look, how you're dressed, how you're not dressed, your weight, etc. All these things don't matter; they only matter in your head, because that's where your focus is. Remember: where your focus goes, your energy flows.

You need to shift your focus off of yourself and direct it onto the audience that you came to serve; onto the message that you came to deliver; onto the value that you came to share.

Anything other than that is you not being yourself. Does that make sense? Get the focus off of you and put the focus back on the people that you would like to serve. This is a crucial shift in mindset.

In conclusion, as one of my friends would say, *"You can't be anybody else, because everyone else is taken, so you have to be yourself."* I also have news for you: When you were born, even if you're one of twins, you came out one at a time. When you were born there were no two people like you. God literally broke the mould. You see, you're unique, you're special, and it's time for you to take on that mantle and embrace yourself.

Don't be afraid to be yourself. I once had a story about a mentor of mine who was delivering an event, and something happened in that event and he came out openly being himself and just expressing what was going on for him. Most people would never ever have said what he said. When I looked back at that scenario and I saw that, I thought wow, incredible. He had no inhibition whatsoever about himself, he felt so free and so comfortable in his own skin with himself that he was able to just express who he is, wow. I got inspiration from that. Now I do the same thing.

The truth is, this speaking malarkey is easy; I'm just myself, whether I'm talking in front of an audience, or I'm talking in front of a camera, it doesn't matter to me. Ultimately, I have something of value to share and I believe in that, and because I believe solely in that, that is the only driving force that I have.

Now, does that mean my presentation is perfect? No, far from it.

Do I make mistakes? Yes absolutely, but it's okay, because I'm not teaching you to be perfect here, I'm teaching you to be conversational. I'm teaching you to be yourself, to be comfortable in your own skin.

There are three main factors that really affect your state as a speaker or presenter.

1. **Focus**: What are you focusing on internally? Where do you put your attention when you are speaking? The only place your focus should be is externally on your audience.

2. **Physiology**: More importantly, your breathing. A lot of newbie speakers and even some professional speakers don't know how to breathe right and perhaps have an awkward breathing pattern or rhythm.

3. **Language**: What are you saying to yourself as you present? Do you say words to affirm how comfortable and how ready you are? Or do you say words that tell you how unprepared you are and how nervous you are? Your performance will be greatly enhanced or worsened by the words (language) you use towards yourself.

I used to be one of these types of speakers; actually, as a matter of fact you may have seen me present before or watched me on YouTube, and I used to stammer. I used to shake and wish the ground would open up and I would sink into it. I could not lead a silent prayer in front of five people. That's how bad I was, and because I'd be shaking, my armpits would be all wet and sweaty. My notes in my hands would also be shaking profusely.

I knew what to say, but the words wouldn't come out because I used to stammer. I wanted to push the words out of my mouth, but they wouldn't come out. Have you ever had a similar experience?

Now, I have developed and trained myself to a level where I know exactly how to get somebody else in the same scenario as me or someone who has never presented before to start presenting with ease, confidence and complete conviction. In other words, you will be, "Speaking and Presenting with IMPACT!"

If I can do it, guess what? You definitely can do the same too!

When I saw my mentors doing it, I started thinking to myself, if they can do that, then I can definitely do it too. The question I had to ask myself was, *"Why am I so hung up on myself?"*

You see, the reason for that is most people take themselves too seriously – and I guess, I was doing the same thing at the time. Perhaps you're doing that right now – Just stop it!

What you need to do instead is to loosen up, relax and smile more and be willing to get things wrong as you are learning and practising and be okay with that. Be willing to fail your way to success.

There was a period when I was having an event, and I was doing a live 3-day Speaking and Presenting with I.M.P.A.C.T training and I had about 6 students in the room. While were training, it was a nice small intimate group. During that time, I was going through a period of detox, and because I was detoxing, it meant that I was releasing a lot of gas - meaning I was farting a lot, just to be frank.

This meant I was going to the toilet a lot as well. I hope you are not reading this while you're having dinner or anything like that, because you are probably wondering, where is this conversation heading, right?

I was standing there in front of the audience and talking to them, and I said, *"Listen guys, by the way, over the next 3 days I'll be going through a detox process and drinking a lot of my green juice, and you can see that I'm drinking greens, super greens as we call them. It means that I'm going to have to be going to the toilet a lot. If you smell anything funny, just know it's me. And I apologise upfront for it."*

They all laughed out loud. You see, I'm comfortable doing that, because I don't want them looking at each other, and going, *"Who did that?"*

There were a couple of occasions in the classroom where I accidentally farted.

Now obviously, if I knew something was coming out of me well in advance then I would excuse myself and go do my business elsewhere (like the toilet or outside the room), right? Unfortunately, these were involuntary reactions. I couldn't control it, because of the detox and it just came out without any warning signs.

So, I said to the students, *"Sorry. By the way, guys, it was me, I did it. You might want to open the windows because this one really stinks you know. It's a silent but deadly one, just open the windows for some fresh air."*

We had fun around it and we joked about it. In some cases if you don't joke about it and talk about it in order to release the tension in the room, it could create a very awkward and uncomfortable situation for both the students and lecturer.

Imagine if you did that and then you kept quiet and kept working, but all the students know you did it because they heard the sound coming from your direction as you are the only one standing there. They'll go, *"He/she just farted... did he/she just fart? Yeah I guess he/she did just farted. Oh my God how rude it is for him/her to just fart like that in the room."*

You know what you've done, you're feeling uncomfortable about it, and therefore that discomfort transfers to your audience. And because you're not addressing it or talking about it, guess what? It lingers on. Something that could be quashed in like thirty seconds now becomes an hour-long conversation: they're talking about it between themselves, and you know you did it. All I'm saying is, there's nothing that can happen in your training room where you can't be yourself. That's about being authentic. When you're able to do that, it just makes you feel relaxed and comfortable in your own skin.

We do it at home with my kids. I mean, we're sitting down and my boys, they do a fart that's really stinky, and I say *"Why didn't you go to the toilet?"* We talk about it, it's done, we just let it go. We don't make a big deal of it.

What I'm saying is, do the same. Be yourself when you're presenting and speaking on stage, and if something goes wrong, acknowledge it. Don't try to hide it. If somebody walks into the room while you're speaking, acknowledge them; that's what my mentor always does. Utilise whatever happens in the room without being afraid to do so. Many speakers are so wired and attached to their content that they have to finish what they're doing, and even though they know something else is going on, they ignore it and just keep focusing on their content and delivery. Well if you're doing that, you're losing your audience, because they know what's happening and you know it too, but you feel too uncomfortable to challenge it or address it in the room right there and then.

Don't ignore things that happen in your presentation room, always address them. It's called using whatever happens in the room to your advantage. I do a lot of speaker training for my mentors all around the world in Malaysia, South Africa, Singapore, Australia, Ukraine, and Romania. I travel around the world doing what I do. Many things often go wrong. Something that has been promised to the audience hasn't been delivered yet. I have to deal with problems and delegates who are not happy with one thing or another, but I'm not going to stand up on stage and then go, *"Oh it's got nothing to do with me, I don't want to talk about that,"* and avoid talking about those things. I address them openly from the platform. Because I'm comfortable within myself, I can deal with it and that is really crucial.

Don't hide from things, be open and expressive about them. It's easier to deal with them openly and honestly than to cover them up and try to hide them.

I'm telling you right now, I've made the mistake of both, and I can tell you which one I prefer to do now. "Be yourself!"

Like I said earlier,

"You have to be yourself, because everyone else is taken."

SUMMARY - Key Points to Remember About Interesting:

- Embrace and accept your awkwardness, weirdness and strange mannerisms because this is what makes you unique and stand out from the rest.
- Determine what style and brand you are and demonstrate that as a speaker.
- Dress comfortably at all times whilst you are speaking or presenting.
- Express yourself honestly, truthfully and authentically.
- Always address the elephant in the room and acknowledge whatever comes up during your presentation.
- Determine what your values are and what you stand for as an individual.
- Know your content and speak unconsciously so you can be more conversational whilst presenting.
- Pay attention to what you focus on, manage your breathing by pausing more and only use positive internal language towards yourself.
- Ultimately, know yourself, be yourself, and be comfortable in your own skin when speaking or presenting to an audience.

CHAPTER 2
MOVEMENT
The Hidden Code Of Natural Presenters

The key to remember here is movement with purpose.

When speaking or presenting, movement plays a vital role in creating real impact experiences for your audience. If done incorrectly, it can come across as distracting and really take the gloss off what could have been a great performance.

Most people who are nervous and twitchy will tend to move up and down frequently for no reason whatsoever. Or they might appear to move their hands a lot or be speaking with a trembling voice or appear to be shaking whilst standing and delivering their talk. As speakers and presenters you have to remember this is not a ping pong game, it's speaking and presenting, so you only move if it's going to add value and impact to your talk, speech or presentation.

Here's what you need to know and understand with regards to movement whilst Speaking and Presenting with IMPACT! Remember the 3 Ps:

"Pace, Plant and Present!"
"Pace, Plant and Present!"
"Pace, Plant and Present!"

Commit that to memory so the next time you are asked to speak or present a subject you pace, pace, pace, you plant your feet where you want to stop, and you present your point or sentence or paragraph before you decide to move again.

So what are the instances where you can move during a presentation?

There are a few clear-cut instances where one can move that will really add tremendous impact to your overall presentation.

- ➢ The larger the audience the more pronounced the movement should be.
  So, let's say you are on a stage speaking to audience of 100+, then you want to move from the centre of the stage to your left-hand-side, then back to the centre of the stage, then you move to the right-hand-side or you can make the movement direct from your left-hand-side to your right-hand-side and back to the middle of the stage. This is generally the main types of movements you should follow throughout your presentation, the idea here being that you get an opportunity to connect with the audience in all the areas around the stage or presentation room. It makes sure no one is left out.
- ➢ The other type of movement that is important is when you are speaking you use your hands to illustrate/emphasise your point/s;
  e.g. "There are three critical things we need to focus on today – And number 1, is X, number 2 is X and finally, number 3 is X." Here you show one finger to represent 1 and 2 fingers to represent 2 and so on and so forth. Another example is using your hands to illustrate how big or small something is. Make sure every movement you do with your hands matches something you've just said to really add impact.

➤ The other area where movement is allowed and encouraged is when you are telling a story, be it your own story or any other story for that matter.

This is where you can get really animated and allow your true personality to shine through. It is great to act out your story, and we call this process, "Show & Tell." There will be more about this later in book 3 of the F1 Speaker System Series, when we come to sharing the art of storytelling within your presentation.

➤ And finally, to really help you look slick and very professional on stage, you need to become aware of the natural movements that you have, and only a handful of professional speakers really use movement deliberately during their presentation.

Below are the six core innate movements we call "archetypes!" These are so important that I'm going to dedicate a whole section to them. Master these innate movements and apply them during your presentation and you will set yourself apart from the rest.

Archetypes

These movements below seem to be perpetuated through the art of storytelling – and they play out in our lives. Archetypes are innate in all of us and we seem to have a natural tendency to use them during conversation and storytelling, like I said. For most people, using archetypes is totally unconscious. Here in these next few pages, I'm going to reveal them to you and make you consciously aware of them. Then it's up to you to practice, practice, practice so you can draw them out at will during your presentations.

The real magic here as a speaker and presenter is: "When you understand and evoke the use of these archetypes from within yourself, then you automatically evoke the same archetypes within your audience!" It's very, very, powerful!

When you evoke a feeling or take on the persona of any one of these archetypes, then your conviction and passion will stir up the same feelings in your audience. This is the difference between just giving a talk and really presenting with IMPACT!

When you learn to master these archetypes, then you become a transformational speaker and presenter that communicates with real authority and confidence.

Here are the six main archetypes when Speaking and Presenting with IMPACT:

1. **The Warrior Gesture**
2. **The Lover Gesture**
3. **The Sage Gesture**
4. **The Jester Gesture**
5. **The Sovereign Gesture**
6. **The Neutral Gesture**

The Warrior Gesture

This is symbolised by the words, "Courage, Strength and Integrity."

The warrior is someone who enforces boundaries and expands boundaries. The gesture that goes with the warrior is putting your right or left hand up and raising your finger next to your thumb up in the air. It looks a bit like a mother scolding her son who has just been naughty, just not pointing directly at someone like a mother does to her children. We raise our hands up and point upwards, like raising a sword up in the air. So, like the warrior, this pose is your symbolic sword.

You should never point your sword at somebody unless you intend to cause the person harm in some way. So, for that very reason, as a speaker you should avoid pointing directly at your audience when adopting the warrior pose.

Using the warrior gesture conveys the status of leadership to you, the speaker, standing in front of your audience or delegates. Just like a general of an army waving his sword aloft in the air to call his troops into action, you too are seen as an authority as your passion and conviction comes across through evoking the warrior archetype within you.

"THE WARRIOR POSE"

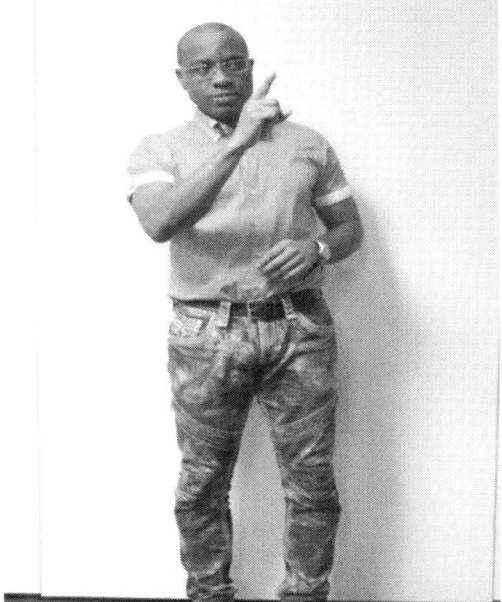

So, what voice tonality do you think matches this particular archetype?

The "VISUAL" tonality, which is fast, quick-paced, loud and emphasises key words and points during your presentation.

Having said that, can you make a point and soften the point? Can you soften the point by using a different tonality? Yes, of course you can by using the soft warrior.

"THE SOFT WARRIOR POSE"

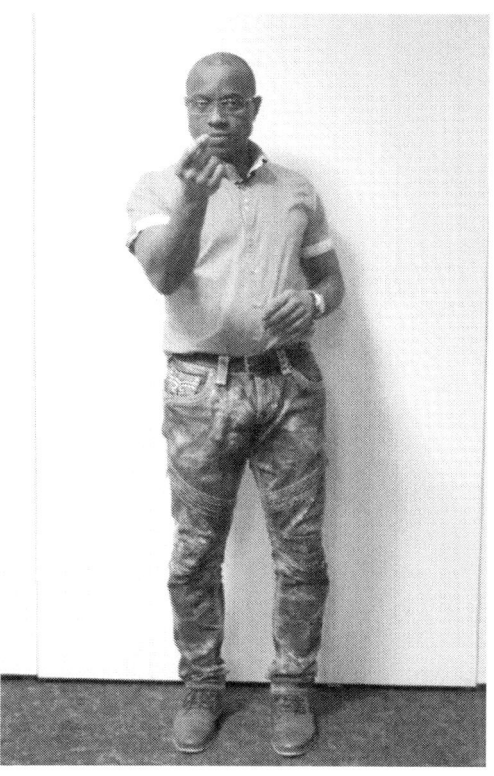

The soft warrior gesture is putting your thumb and your second finger of either hand together and raising your hand in the air like the picture above indicates. Or this time you can actually point the soft warrior directly at someone and it doesn't look as aggressive and does not feel like you are attacking the person with your point or word. Most politicians use the soft warrior. To avoid becoming overbearing and too domineering use the soft warrior to soften a word or point a bit to help temper its effects.

Usage of the Warrior Gesture

- ➤ The main use of the warrior gesture is to ultimately call your troops (audience/delegates) to take some form of action as a result of hearing you speak or present.
- ➤ Use it to punch out your message by emphasising certain key words or phrases during your presentation.
- ➤ You most definitely want to use the warrior gesture a lot towards the end of your presentation because it will certainly help to call your army (audience/delegates) to action so they can act on your message.

The Lover Gesture

This is symbolised by the words, "Open, Trustworthy and Vulnerable."

The lover is open, vulnerable, trusting and speaks from the heart. When you are evoking this archetype during your presentation, it will allow your audience to be more open, trusting and vulnerable too. In a way, it gives them permission to feel the same feelings as you. So, they are more open and receptive to your message, and more importantly they believe in you and trust what you are saying.

This is the lover movement, open palms outstretched, elbows lowered slightly. Make sure your outstretched open palms are above your waist, just like you see in the picture below. Now you shouldn't leave your hands out there for too long, otherwise it looks a bit weird. It's a very quick and smooth up and down motion, a bit like standing in front of a large window and you touch it with your open palms outstretched in front of you and then you put them down.

"THE LOVER POSE"

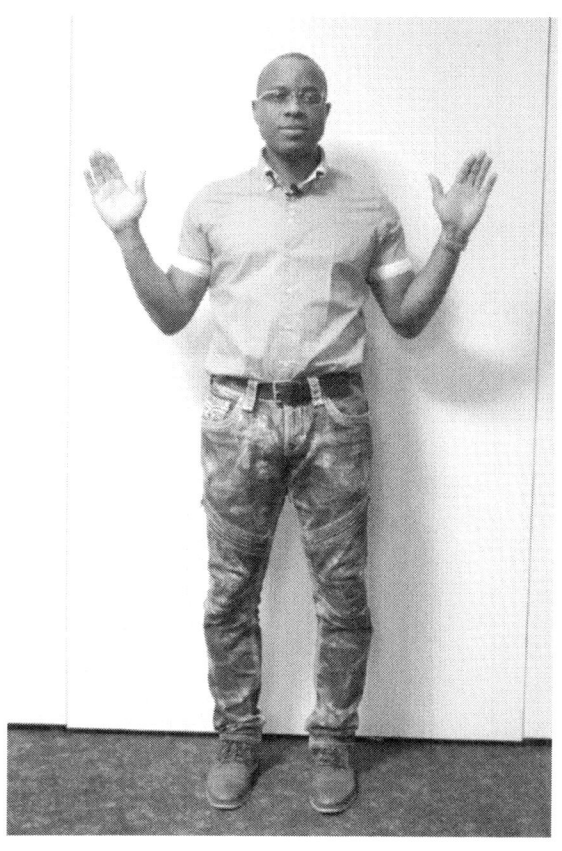

One of the reasons why this works is because when people see your palms, it makes you appear more trustworthy. They trust you more because we take in a lot of information when we shake someone's hand. We take in the grip or whether someone's hand is cold, warm, soft or hard, etc. The challenge of course is when you are presenting and speaking to an audience of 100 plus. You don't go around shaking everyone's hand. So instead, we show the audience the love signal by showing the palms of our hands. This replaces the handshake for you as the speaker.

Usage of the Lover Gesture

- The main use of the lover archetype is to convey the message of openness and trust to your audience. You most definitely want to use this movement a lot at the beginning of your presentation. It certainly helps to boost your relationship with the audience.

- Another important fact to note here is, if you like to wear long-sleeved shirts whilst presenting, then you need to take off your cufflinks or unbutton your cuffs and fold up your sleeves to reveal your forearms. You see, if open palms represent being open and trustworthy then revealing your forearms represents even more trust. Many years ago, we didn't shake hands; we actually used to shake forearms to check that the other person was not concealing any daggers. So, most often when you see me speak, I will have my sleeves rolled up to reveal my forearms for this very reason. So, there you have it; the lover sign illustrates that you the speaker are honest, authentic, genuine and a normal, regular person who can be trusted and believed.

The Sage Gesture

This archetype is symbolised by these words, "Truth, Knowledge, Wisdom, Connection and Sharing." The sage is an individual who is searching for truth, knowledge and wisdom. They are leaders who have mastered their craft in order to share it. They share their truth, knowledge and wisdom, not those who gain knowledge and wisdom and use it to make a statement of superiority over others; that isn't the sage I'm talking about. As a speaker and presenter, you always want to share your expertise with others because you believe strongly in the value that you provide, and you know that when you share it with others it will improve them in some shape or form.

When you evoke the sage archetype within yourself whilst speaking, it shows you as the authority, mentor, wise one, guide and the person who is looking to be instrumental in someone else's life.

You will see a lot of politicians and true professional public speakers using this pose, like president Bill Clinton, Barack Obama, Tony Blair, Tony Robbins, Brian Tracy and Zig Ziglar, just to mention a few.

So, what is the gesture for the sage archetype? I thought you'd never ask! Now, it doesn't matter which hand you use, and with your thumb and second finger grab hold of your chin. Some people put both the thumb and second finger on the same side of the chin. This is okay, but it looks like they are pondering over something or deliberating what to do next. Conversely, if you extend your thumb and second finger and grab your chin with the thumb and second finger holding onto your chin from either side, it makes you look more certain. Then your spare arm (right or left, depending on which hand you decide to hold the chin with) will go across your body, and with that hand make a fist and rest the elbow of the opposite arm on top of your fist. See the picture below; it's a really nice confident pose.

"THE SAGE POSE"

Usage of the Sage Gesture

> ➢ The main use of the sage archetype is to convey to your audience that you are an expert in the area in which you teach and that you really know your stuff.

➢ It is also a very useful pose to use when taking questions from your audience. It buys you time to think and consider the question before answering it. What do I mean? Well, as a speaker, get into the habit of repeating word for word any questions you are asked by your audience. This will allow everyone to hear what the question was, as it might relate to them or be similar to what they wanted to ask. More importantly, it buys you valuable seconds of thinking time. The person who asked the question also feels appreciated as they feel you are taking your time to really consider the question before you answer it.

➢ It is a great gesture to use when someone is sharing their story, a statement of fact or history that is related to a timeline. For instance, something that happened in the past, something that is happening in this present time or something that is going to happen in the future, e.g. "25 years ago I came to the UK"; "What am I doing now? That is a great question, what I am doing now is…"; and finally, "Did you know in 2020 the world is going to change dramatically for the better? Let me elaborate…" This is a great pose to have in those moments.

The Jester Gesture

This archetype is symbolised by these words, "Joy, Fun, Freedom of Expression, Spontaneity, Variety, Excitement and Enthusiasm."

This is the fun side of you coming out on stage, the part of your being that is joyous and feels totally free on stage to express your authentic self. It is any gesture which is unsymmetrical. It could be any movement at all, like both hands expressed outwardly, where one hand is up and the other is down, as if to say you are telling a joke of some sort. Or it could just be your head and facial expressions, like one eyebrow raised and the other lowered or both raised. See the picture below:

"THE JESTER POSE"

It's the classical gesture for appearing or looking like a fool on stage. It conveys a message that you are entertaining, and you don't take yourself too seriously, which allows your audience to really warm to you. By being in the Jester pose you also give your audience permission to have fun with you.

In ancient history, what was the role of the jester at court? The jester's role was to amuse the king and also to temper the ego of the king. We could say that the jester got away with murder. He was the only one who got away with stuff that others would get beheaded for, because he was seen as the king's personal comedian.

When used appropriately, this movement can also allow you to get away with murder – and by that I mean things that would normally upset your audience will have them applauding you for saying it rather than getting you in deep waters. It also helps if you have built up a sufficient amount of rapport with your audience before attempting to say something controversial whilst using this gesture.

Usage of the Jester Gesture

- It's very useful when you are telling a joke or saying something funny.
- It's a great gesture for telling stories that really captivate your audience. In storytelling it is the "Show & Tell" aspect of the story that really makes it come alive. Bring the audience into your world and allow them to relate to you on a deeper level. Totally express your emotions throughout the process of your story; there will be more about this later during the Storytelling section.
- It amplifies the comedian in you.
- It's used to temper your own ego so you don't take yourself too seriously.
- It makes you come across to your audience as someone who is entertaining and fun to be around.
- It also allows you to let yourself off the hook and to be okay with not being Mr/Mrs Perfect. In other

words, it's okay to make mistakes and not have all the answers.

The Sovereign Gesture

This archetype is symbolised by these words, "Peaceful, Authority, Majestic, Certainty, Wisdom, Facts and Truth."

The sovereign is the ruler, but they rule from a place of peaceful majesty. The sovereign archetype is the one who is able to share statements of facts, truth and calm situations down with total presence and leadership.

The correct posture for this archetype is palms down with both hands; it's a bit like trying to lay a shirt nice and smoothly on an ironing board. See the picture below for full details:

"THE SOVEREIGN POSE"

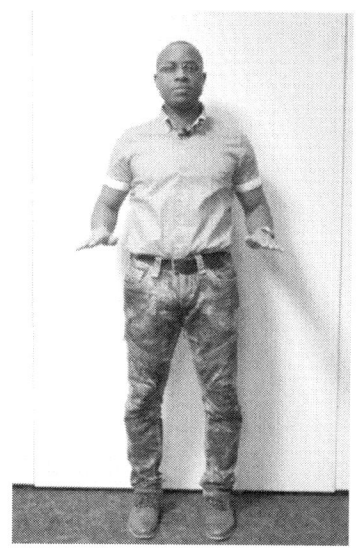

Usage of the Sovereign Gesture

> It is useful for making factual statements, things that are undeniably true. For example, "This is the way it is… And it's not going to change for you or anyone!" or, "Life is for living, and to live you have to give that which you seek to have, period."

> It allows you to assert your authority is a very calm and measured way without making you out to be a dictator or authoritarian.

> It also allows you to emphasise certain words and punch, them out in a calm and assured manner.

So, what do you do with your hands when you are not using any of the 5 archetypes mentioned above? You adopt the neutral pose.

The Neutral Gesture

This archetype is symbolised by these words, "Balanced, Poised, Composed." The sign for the neutral gesture is you pretend to hold a tiny piece of paper with both sets of fingers, just in front of your belly button, and ensure that your hands are nice and relaxed. See the picture below for the correct pose:

"THE NEUTRAL POSE"

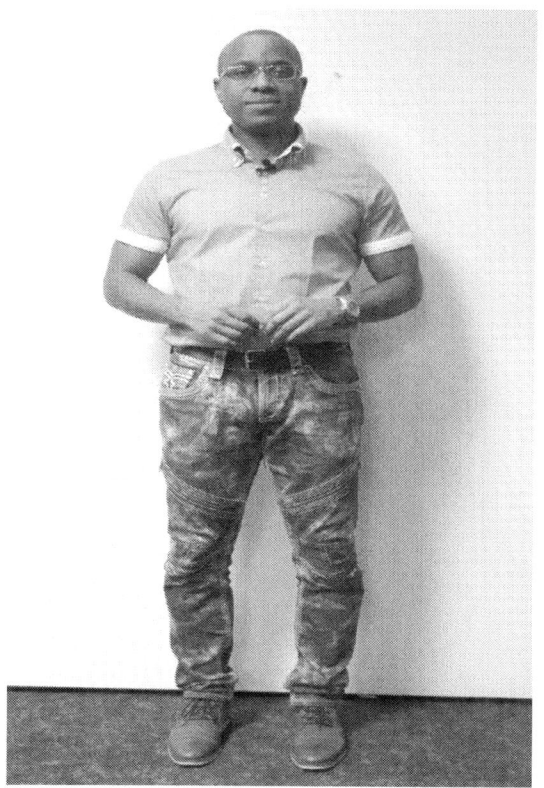

Usage of the Neutral Gesture

- ➤ It makes you stand out from your fellow professional speakers, making you appear more professional, polished and grounded.
- ➤ It makes it easy to transition between the other archetype movements like the warrior, lover, sage, jester and sovereign.
- ➤ It's your central point where you start from and move out of into another gesture and move back to.

SUMMARY - Key Points to Remember About Movement:

➢ Don't overuse the same gesture.
➢ Always go back to neutral when not in 'show and tell' or gesturing.
➢ Don't move all the time; remember, pace, plant and present. Stillness is very powerful, especially when you are delivering your impact line, golden nugget, take away, keep phrase or foundational messages.
➢ Use your characters' gestures, especially when telling a story.
➢ Let your emotions drive you; show and tell 360 degrees.
➢ Use bigger gestures for bigger audiences.
➢ Have an animated face, meaning use your facial expressions whilst speaking or presenting to enhance or exaggerate the point you're making. It is worth practicing in front of the mirror using all your facial muscles.
➢ Make smiling your main gesture and ensure you adopt it throughout your presentation if possible. This is especially important if you are speaking live to a camera or doing a live video recording.

The key to movement is, you have to move on purpose and deliberately, otherwise don't move at all.

CHAPTER 3
PRESENCE
Show Up 100% Every Time You Speak

This next point is very important. I'm serious here; without this, forget everything else, well obviously apart from being yourself, because you have to be yourself, but this is key right here. It's actually on par with knowing yourself and being yourself. It's the difference that makes a difference. If you don't have this one, don't bother showing up to do a webinar, a video, a seminar, or an event. Whatever it may be for you, just don't bother, because it's not going to work. What am I talking about? I'm talking about presence.

Now, what do I mean by presence?

Well within presence there are three elements here.

1. It is about managing your emotional state.

    You do this by taking care of 3 factors that affect your state:

"SPEAKER STATE"

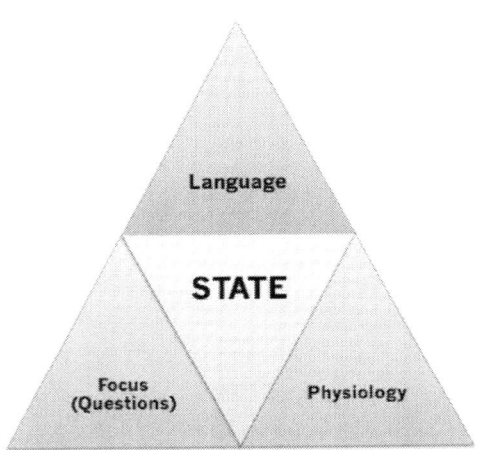

You manage what you focus on (only focus on an outstanding performance every single time) by asking yourself the relevant questions, and you use only positive language towards yourself. With physiology you maintain a good stance but more importantly, you maintain a good breathing pattern or rhythm. This will help to keep you in a positive state.

2. It's about your physicality, your stance, how you stand on stage:

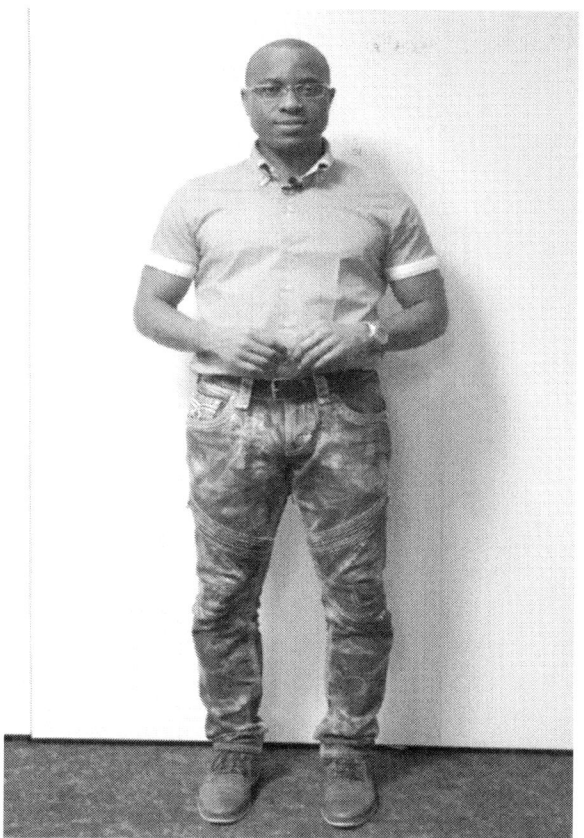

3. It is about the energy that you bring onto the stage:

   A speaker's energy must be open and positive on stage at all times. Your body, breath, voice, mind, heart and spirit must all be in sync (meaning working in unity) to support your performance.

You see, these three components are crucial to you speaking and presenting with real impact.

If you don't have these three elements showing up for you, well, it's a bit like playing poker with my friends and they say,

"Either you go hard, or you go home." It's the same thing here. Either you show up or you stay at home, literally. You can't turn up to give a presentation, webinar, seminar, or video without any presence.

Can you imagine I just walk up here, and I teach you all of these modules and I'm sluggish and slouched, with my head down facing the floor and my energy is non-existent and my confidence and self-esteem are very low?

My voice and body language would come across very poorly and you'd be asking yourselves, *"Why on God's Earth did I get up for this loser? He's so boring."*

This is how some presenters and speakers show up to perform. They show up to deliver their events, presentations or seminars with absolutely no presence whatsoever. They're not present, it's like ... floppy body language. There's no energy in them and they're walking around as though they're carrying the weight and troubles of the whole world on their shoulders. You can't do that as a professional speaker. You've got to hold yourself up in a whole different stance.

You see, we used to run an event called Miss Universe Norfolk. It is part of the Miss Universe GB, and Donald Trump used to run the Miss Universe beauty pageant, but I think he has given it up and some other organisations run it now. Anyway, basically every year, we'll have a girl contestant from all the regions around the UK become Miss Universe GB. I usually did train and coach that contestant, and then she went on to represent Great Britain at Miss Universe at the big global event abroad.

At that time, my ex-partner and I used to run one of the regional heats for Miss Universe Norfolk, and we would typically have about 200 contestants enter the competition at the regional heats level.

That number then quickly gets narrowed down by a process of elimination to about 26 contestants who progress to the Regional Competition Finals, a big event usually held at Dunston Hall in Norwich. There are usually about 250 people attending the event.

It's a big show, a big stage and three rounds of competition. First, the catwalk round, then the bikini round, which is rounded off by the main, evening gown, round. It's a really fantastic occasion and at the end of the day, we will have a first runner up, second runner up and a winner for that competition. That winner will then go on to compete on the Miss Universe GB stage. Ultimately if she wins there, she eventually represents the whole of Great Britain, basically.

At these events we used to train all these contestants on interview skills, and how to hold themselves with confidence. We had a role-model who would come in to show the contestants how to catwalk on stage (usually an ex-winner of the competition). When you're on stage participating as a contestant and doing your catwalk, you have to hold everything in. You have to hold your stomach in, you have to hold your derrière/behind in, and you have everything all tight and poised and when walking, you walk with that elegance. Everything's held in, it's all part of the show. As a speaker, you have presence on the stage because you have to possess a similar stance where you switch yourself on. You can't be sluggish and slow on stage or on set without any energy, or more crucially, not using all of your available height because your head is facing down.

As a speaker, you want to maintain a good stance (check the picture above), which is: legs hip-width apart, shoulders nice and straight, head straight ahead and looking down at the camera if you're filming a video or looking down at your audience if you're presenting. Not looking up at the ceiling or looking down at the stage or floor - and your hands should be in the neutral position (refer to the movement section above); right on your belly button is your gauge for your hands. Now you could do this in many ways, and some people do the stipple hand gesture. I don't really like this; it stands out too much for me and can be distracting to the audience, or sometimes I hold the fingers in between each other, not clasped tightly but very loose and relaxed. Too tight and it makes you look like you're a nervous presenter.

One of my mentors holds one of their fingers of their left hand with their right hand, just nice and relaxed. Again, around your belly button, just nice and relaxed on stage, and this gives you presence. You can walk around, you can move around, you can tell a story, you can tell a joke or be joking around with your audience, but the minute you start presenting content again make sure you're in the neutral position.

Men typically stand in a macho position when speaking on stage. They have their legs wide apart, accentuating their private area on display. Or they sometimes stand like a cowboy, with their feet like at ten to one on a clock face. See the pictures below:

"TYPICAL STANCE FOR MEN"

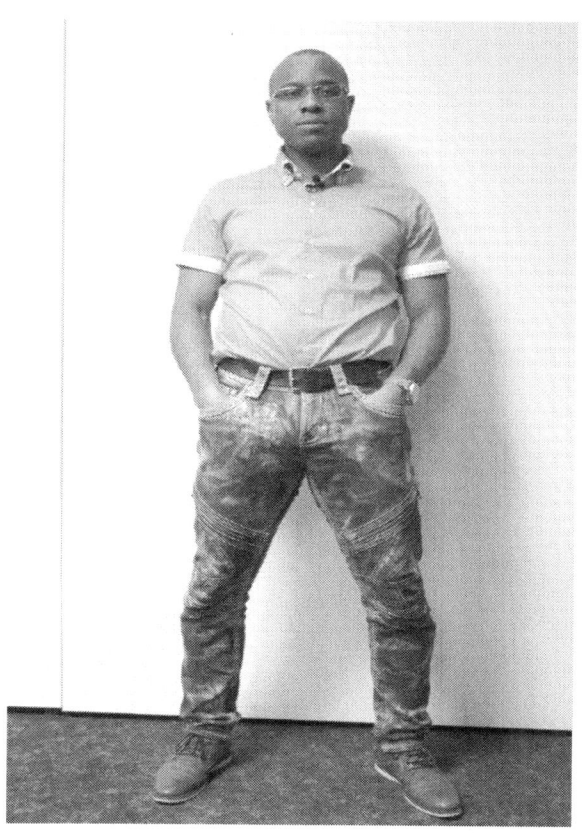

"THE COWBOY STANCE"

Ladies have a completely different stance to men. They do something very weird with their hips when standing. They start resting on one hip of either their right or left leg and then after a while they swap feet and rest on the other hip of the left or right leg.

"TYPICAL STANCE FOR WOMEN"

This makes them look shifty as they keep shifting from one hip to another. The challenge with this is, it's not a very good look for presenting or speaking. People won't take you seriously, so do exactly as I have outlined above to maintain a proper stance and presence on stage, for both men and women, whilst presenting and speaking.

The only reason why women do this shifty stance is to express their sexuality to men, and men find this very attractive in a woman. It also makes them appear to take a less dominant position to men whilst they are out as a couple, which is absolutely fine in those circumstances, but definitely not on stage. Especially if you want to be taken seriously and you want people to listen to your message and not just watch your assets on display.

So, that is your stance, your physicality; the way you present yourself is very important.

The other critical factor that affects your emotional state is breathing. What do I mean? You are not pausing enough whilst speaking. A lot of rookie speakers don't pause at all or nowhere near enough. You see, when you're speaking, it involves breathing out, and that presupposes you must take a breath in at some point or you're in trouble… right? My speaker mentor usually gets us to do an exercise. You might want to go ahead and try it out for yourself too. Put your hand out in front of you and read the alphabet A, B, C, D, E, and as you're speaking, the air is coming out of your mouth, which means when you're speaking, you're breathing out. So, when you're not speaking you should be taking a breath in, right? If you are not then you'll run out of breath very quickly, which is not a good thing as a speaker.

You see, what happens is most people just talk too quickly and they don't pause enough, they don't stop for air. You want to pause for two reasons. One, you want to pause so that your audience can really take in what you're saying, because if you're just talking all the time, they'll miss it. They can't relate it to themselves. They can't really see how what you're saying can change what they're doing to improve their lives. Pause, and let them take it in. the other reason why you want to pause is that it will give you time to just breathe in, and when you're speaking, make sure you are drinking lots of water as well. The reason why you want to do that is sometimes when you start speaking and your mouth is dry, you start hearing this tacky sound, and that is your tongue sticking to the roof of your mouth. That's the tacky sound you hear. It's not a very nice sound when you're speaking.

You don't want to be hearing that, so you want to make sure that you're well lubricated by drinking lots of water.

Even if you drank a lot of water beforehand, make sure that before you step on stage, before you do your webinar, before you record your videos, just drink a glass of water. Just a small glass of water, lubricate your mouth and your tongue and let saliva build up in your mouth, which is nice, rather than having a dry mouth whilst speaking. This is a very, very important tip. During my live speaker training when I'm talking about pausing, somebody would invariably ask me this question, *"How long should you pause for?"* And perhaps you are asking the same question in your own minds as you are reading this book now.

The answer is simple: you pause for as long as you feel uncomfortable and then you pause some more.

You see, you can pause for as long as you want. Again, during live training I would demonstrate this to the audience in the room. I would pause, pause, pause, pause, pause, and pause some more and then keep pausing for about 30 – 45 seconds then I would say, *"Now you don't know whether I've just paused for effect or I've paused because I can't remember what the freaking hell I was going to say next, right?"* They usually all laugh at this stage, but it definitely proves my point.

It doesn't matter how long you pause for, just make sure that you pause, because it probably allows your audience to relate to you and what you are saying to them. It also allows you time to catch up with your train of thought to then carry on. Remember, think fast and talk slowly, with regular pauses.

SUMMARY - Key Points to Remember About Presence:

- Presence is the difference that makes a difference.
- The two main factors that affect your state as a speaker are your physicality, the way you stand and your breathing patterns. Learn to find your rhythm as a speaker.
- Show up 100%, not 99%. You are either present or not there at all. No half measures here.
- Learn to pause more whilst speaking, it will assist you on two counts. One, it will allow your audience to think and relate to what you are saying and secondly, it will allow you time to gather your thoughts.
- Remember, think fast and speak slowly, so you find your own tempo and rhythm and maintain it.
- Maintain an upright stance so you can use all of your available height whilst presenting.
- Your energy is very important for being present. Remember, the energy you show up with is the energy your audience will pick up on.
- Express yourself emotionally – meaning use your body and facial expressions to convey your message.

CHAPTER 4
AWARENESS
How to Shift the Mood of Your Audience

This chapter is focused on you as a presenter and your ability to calibrate your audience at any given time and change the mood or energy in your presentation room. This is what I call, "Awareness!"

You have to have the ability to be absolutely 100% aware of your audience at all times. By awareness, I mean you've got to know where you're at, and you get to know where your audience is at in terms of their energy levels. If you're not aware of it, you as a speaker cannot change it. I'm sure you will agree with that, right?

If you're not aware of your audience's state, you can't manage it. And if you are not aware of your own state, what chance do you have of managing your audience's state or mood?

Awareness is about calibrating the whole audience and the room you are in.

Let me ask you this: If you're looking at a painting, do you look at just one aspect of that painting, or do you see the whole painting? Which one?

Well, you're right, you see the whole painting. The question is, why wouldn't you as a speaker be aware of your whole entire room, since the whole entire room is the painting? You want to be calibrating the whole entire room. Even if you're talking on a webinar or online, you also need engagement. Your audience can engage with you by you asking them questions and saying, *"Okay, does that makes sense to you? Let me see the hands symbol flashing on the screen. Or just simply type 'Yes' in the comments section so I can see that this is making sense to you. Great, thank you."*

You're still engaging them, okay? You want to be aware of your audience at all times. Awareness is crucial, and I see a lot of speakers that miss this point. They're just not aware. They care more about their content than their audience because they're stuck to their notes, and whatever else is happening in the room, they just ignore it like it's not happening. You can't do that as a speaker. You've got to be aware of everything that's happening in your training room, and utilise it to your advantage, making sure that you're utilising everything that happens. The French call this act *"Utilisation"*. You want to utilise whatever is going on in your training room and in your workshop, so that you're using it to your advantage.

I'm always aware if someone walks into the room or if someone yawns or if someone sneezes or someone coughs or if someone is heckling or if someone has farted in the room because I'm always calibrating the room throughout my presentation. You, as a speaker and a presenter, want to be doing the same thing during your presentations.

The question you might be asking now is, *"How do you do that?"*

Great question! We calibrate our audience's mood and state by using a method called "Expanded Awareness" or "Peripheral Vision."

Let me explain:

You pick a spot and you focus on it, excluding everything else, and whilst maintaining your focus on that one spot, you slowly begin to expand your awareness and start to notice everything else. The idea here is as a speaker, whilst speaking to an individual in your presentation room, you are also still aware of the rest of the room by using your peripheral vision.

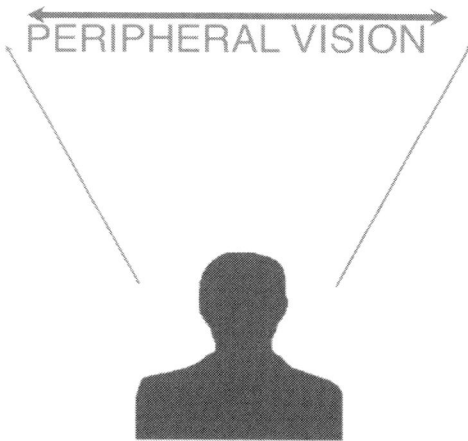

Most speakers use Fovial vision (focusing only on one thing at a time) as opposed to peripheral vision or expanded awareness.

Why is this important?

Awareness is vital, especially when people have just come back from lunch and you see that the energy is sagging and they're feeling sleepy. Now, if one person yawns, or two people yawn, that's okay. If I'm calibrating and I'm seeing 1, 2, 3, 4, 5, 6 people yawning in a room of 30 or 40 people, then I've got to do something about it. And because I'm totally aware of it, I know exactly what to do to change the energy or mood in the room. Does that make sense?

As a speaker or presenter, you need to be aware of this and know exactly what to do to change the energy or mood in the room.

How do you change up the room once the energy or mood levels have dropped?

The first step is to be aware that the energy levels have dropped. Then the second step is to get people up and moving their bodies radically in some way. You better have a few icebreaker exercises up your sleeve that you can use to energise your audience or change their state as a professional speaker. You need that, that's crucial. I have a few icebreakers up my sleeve. It could be a few games, it could be just a simple massage, some music just to get them going and having fun. Have a few things that they can do, that you can utilise to change the audience's state in the room. It's very, very important. Even if you're on a webinar and you find you're not getting many responses, you could say a few things that could engage them and get them responding to you, so that you know that they're actually listening and they're with you; it's very important that you do that. Perhaps, send them a challenge that they can complete at the end of the webinar or promise them something they will need but only provide it to those who stay with you till the end of the webinar. This will keep them alert and attentive for the reward or incentive at the end.

Awareness is an essential piece here, because if you're not aware of your audience, you've lost them. Anything less than being aware of your audience, and you've lost them completely. The whole point of us engaging them at a deeper level is we want to get their attention and want to keep it and hold it for longer. When they see us do a change of step, they'll go, *"Oh my God he's so aware, he knows that. Oh, I just feel a bit tired after lunch and he's just changed it up, now I feel a little bit more energised"*. They're more awake and they'll thank you for it.

Don't be afraid to change up the energy in the room. Use your own sensory acuity and be aware of your audience in the room - especially the energy levels if they drop or increase. This is especially important when you're about to call them to action. You can't do that when the energy levels are low; you need an energetic state. You really need to make sure that the room is energised and they're with you, especially when you're doing your call to action or doing your close. This is very, very, important.

There you have it, awareness, be aware of your audience.

You need to expand your awareness beyond the individual to the entire room.

SUMMARY - Key Points to Remember About Awareness:

➢ Awareness is about calibrating the entire room.
➢ Manage your state so you can focus your attention on your audience's state.
➢ Research various ways in which you can help change your audience's mood and state.
➢ Utilise whatever shows up or happens in the room during your presentation to your advantage.
➢ You need to expand your awareness beyond the individual to the entire room using the skills of peripheral vision or expanded awareness.

CHAPTER 5
CONNECTION
The Secret To Making Your Audience Feel Special

This next point you might find a bit amusing.

It's a very peculiar one, because when I've discussed it with a few delegates in my training classes, they've been taught in one particular way, and when they pick up the strategy from me, they go, *"Oh my God, that's scary"*. They've never been taught how to do this.

What's scary is the fact that they're not doing it, that's what's scary!

What's actually exciting is, when they learn how to do it, they actually enjoy it and it is no longer scary.

What am I talking about?

I'm talking about connection with your audience. Connecting with your audience.

What do I mean by connection?

Well here I'm specifically talking about eye contact. Do you want to make your audience feel special? I know I do, and you should too.

How do you make your audience feel special?

Let me ask you this: If somebody's worth talking to, are they worth looking at?

You're damn right they are. Why aren't you doing it? You see, some people have this school of thought that when you're speaking in public and you're talking to a large audience, rather than looking at each individual face, look above their heads, and talk to the back of the room. Really?

I had this experience once. I was teaching my 3-day Speaking and Presenting with I.M.P.A.C.T to a bunch of young children, teenagers and adults from the age of 8 years up to 30 years old. This was for a charity group, and I had an 8-year-old girl saying, *"At school when I was speaking, my teacher told me that I shouldn't look at people's eyes directly. Instead, I should look above them at the back of the room and not look directly at their eyes".*

I was like, *"Honey, when you and I are talking, are you looking at me?"* She goes, *"Yes."* *"Well when you're speaking to your audience you should be looking at them."* I'm saying the same to you. That is just BS (the teacher's belief system) - you need to be looking at your audience. It's crucial that you look at your audience while you are speaking to them, because why wouldn't you?

Here's the key: If you want to make your audience feel significant and special, then you need to look at them. You need to make eye contact with them and be comfortable with that eye contact. Now sometimes you might look at somebody in your audience and they might look away, but don't let that person be you, let it be your audience. Let them be the uncomfortable one; you shouldn't be uncomfortable looking directly in their eyes. If you are uncomfortable looking at them, forget it. I think we will all agree that connection is not scanning the room and only making eye contact for one second, two seconds or three seconds and then you're off again quickly looking at someone else for three seconds? Just scanning the room and not really connecting with your audiences that's not connection. Connection here means, connecting with somebody and having a conversation with them. Looking into their eyes as you are speaking to them and really connecting with them deeply.

When you're done having that conversation, pick somebody else out in your audience and have a conversation with that person. As you're talking to them, make sure you're connecting with them long enough to make eye contact, for 15 - 20 seconds or longer in some cases depending on how long the particular statement that you're making lasts for. Then connect with somebody else that you're talking to, and make eye contact with them, and connect with them until you feel that train of thought, sentence or paragraph is complete, whatever the case may be for you, and do this randomly throughout the room. I'm not talking about doing it in a linear fashion, as in talking to people in a row and then the next row, etc. That's boring, it's not like that. It's really random; you talk to somebody at the back of the room, you talk to somebody in the front of the room, you talk to somebody over on your right-hand-side, you talk to somebody over on your left-hand-side. Come back to the front of the room and talk to somebody there.

Randomly, pick people out in your audience. Now in an audience of about 30, 100, 200, 300, 400, even 1,000 and I've got an hour to speak, I will literary see the majority of those people. They will have connected with me one on one. It is powerful; it really makes your audience feel special. They connect to you, and they feel as if you're just talking to them, but you're not because you're talking to everybody else in the room. If I'm having a conversation with somebody in the front of the room, I'm talking to this person in the front row, and I'm connected with them, guess what? The whole audience is zoned into the conversation, they're listening to this conversation going on and they're actually more attentive to what's going on there than if I was talking to everyone and ignoring them. It's very powerful, and I want you to remember that.

Connection is really powerful and maintaining eye contact with people in your audience makes them really feel special and you will really connect with them. Smile while you do it, make smiling your standard gesture, but don't always smile all the time. You will look a bit contrived if you're just smiling all the time. Smile naturally, and even if you're not smiling and showing your teeth, smile with your eyes like Tara Banks would say, *"smile with your eyes"*. Have a softer approach. Some of you are presenting but you're so serious. Have a soft look on your face. Relax all the muscles in your face. Look as if you're looking at your newborn baby. Look as if you're looking at a loved one. Have that look; it makes you more attractive and allows you to relax when you're connecting with your audience. People will find you more attractive and more charismatic as well. Try it out next time you are presenting. It really works.

Connection is important, because here is the thing: without truly connecting with your audience, what's the point? The whole point of you sharing your message is to connect with the individual people in the room, so that they can connect with you. That all starts with you looking at your audience when you are speaking to them. When you're delivering your presentation, make sure you're maintaining eye contact with every single individual in the room, even if you're talking to an audience of 10,000. They'll have big screens on the stage, on either side of it. When you look to the camera and you're speaking to the back of the room, they will see your eye contact at the back of the room looking straight at them as well. Look down the lens of the camera and speak to them now and again and they'll connect with you as well. There's no excuse for not connecting with everyone in the audience.

All right, there you have it: connection.

Eye contact with your audience gives you access into their soul to make a deeper connection with them. As they say, the "EYES" have it!

CONNECTION

SUMMARY - Key Points to Remember About Connection:

- ➢ Make smiling your standard gesture.
- ➢ Select people in your audience to look at randomly.
- ➢ Direct your eye contact from the front of the room, to the back of the room, to the left of the room and to the right of the room.
- ➢ Hold your gaze for about 15-20 seconds or more in some cases, at least until you finish your train of thought with that person. Then select a different audience member.
- ➢ When you are speaking to a large audience of 5,000 – 10,000, you will need to occasionally look at the camera straight ahead of you and speak directly to it. As the audience looks at you, they will feel that you are looking directly into their eyes, especially when you are presenting.
- ➢ Make your audience feel special, unique and valuable by connecting with them individually during your presentation.

CHAPTER 6
TONALITY

How Do You Engage Your Audience with Your Voice?

Last but not least, this part of this module is a very powerful one. This is also the reason why people will listen to you for a longer period of time.

Let me ask you this question - do you like to listen to a monotonous speaker? Yes or no? Well you don't have to answer that because I know the answer. It's absolutely no. You don't want to listen to a monotonous speaker. Here's my advice: don't be one yourself.

We're talking about tonality, but what do I mean by tonality?

I'm talking about your vocal inflection. How you use your voice and vary your tone when speaking and presenting.

Let me introduce you to The Charisma Pattern:

"THE CHARISMA PATTERN"

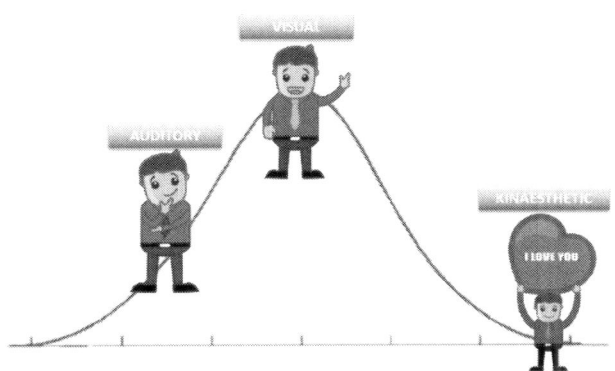

The Charisma Pattern is very useful because it puts a heartbeat into your presentation since you are making full use of your vocal range by using your Auditory voice, Visual voice and your Kinaesthetic voice combined throughout your presentation.

It's a bit like an E.C.G. machine that a sick patient would be hooked up to in a hospital. If the patient is still alive, the E.C.G. machine moves in an up and down fashion to indicate a heartbeat in the patient – meaning there's life in them. But if the patient dies, then the machine just produces a straight line with the same hideous tone consistently, indicating a loss of life.

Most speakers out there are monotonous speakers because they are just flat lining, no heartbeat in their presentations.

So, how do you know if you're a monotonous speaker?

Here's how you know if you're a monotonous speaker, you'll be doing one of three things.

1. You'll be just using your Auditory voice alone, and after a while it becomes monotonous to your audience:

AUDITORY

Medium Pace
Rhythmical
Clarity

2. You'll be just using your Visual voice alone and after a while it becomes monotonous to your audience:

VISUAL

Fast, Loud, Punchy

3. You'll be just using your Kinaesthetic voice alone and after a while it becomes monotonous to your audience:

KINAESTHETIC

Slow, Quiet, Heartfelt,
Breathy, lots of Pauses

TONALITY

You see, the Charisma Pattern involves the Auditory voice, which is The Sage if you like, or the Visual voice which is The Warrior or the Kinaesthetic voice which is The Lover.

This means that you start at a neutral place here (auditory), and then you take them high(visual) and then you bring them low(kinaesthetic). You get it? It's especially good if you use the Charisma Pattern when you're telling stories. You must vary your voice and take your audience on a journey, up and down with you. It's that change in tonality of your vocal inflection that keeps them sitting on the edge of their seats and listening to your every word.

A really good demonstration of that is my story where I talk about my Dad. My natural sounding voice is about 50 or 60% on the Auditory, but I would occasionally, switch to my visual voice, and occasionally, switch to my kinaesthetic voice, moving my tone up and down, and it goes on like that to keep a heartbeat in my speech.

So, if you ever want to see a demonstration of me telling my story about my Dad, check out our YouTube channel.

On the video, you will see and hear me using my Dad's voice in a visual tone saying, *"Sons, I have just received this letter, from your, boarding school... Unfortunately, I can't afford to send you to school, because they're saying we owe a lot of money, and I can't afford it".*

On the same video you will hear me speaking, sharing my internal dialogue with the audience and asking my Dad a question with the kinaesthetic tone saying, *"Oh gosh, if I don't go to school, what am I going to do? I need to ask him. Dad, if I don't go to school what do you want me to do?"*

And finally, on the same video you will hear me using my Dad's voice in a visual tone responding to my question above

"I don't care what you do, you can go and become a welder, a bricklayer or a carpenter, take your pick. I really don't care what you do, I can't afford to send you to school anymore, end of discussion. Go and seat down."

You see, just in that little dialogue above you can hear the contrast in my tone of voice, when I'm being my Dad using the visual or warrior voice tonality. Verse being myself in a state of shock, and worry using the kinaesthetic or lover voice tonality. There's a big contrast between the two, and you want to be doing that yourself. It's very important.

Can you imagine someone speaking just in one tone throughout their presentation? For example, there was a YouTube video of a guy giving a speech about a company, I think it was Microsoft or Apple. They asked this guy to make a speech, and he got up and he said, *"I love this company, I love this company, I love this company. This company is the very, very best. I love this company! I love this company!"* He was just shouting and screaming. People were thinking, "Oh my God, is he going to stop?" That's just a little bit too much. Then we have other people who are just in the Kinaesthetic zone, being a monotonous speaker, and they're just speaking in that same voice all the time.

For me this is quite funny because I have a lot of friends, as a trainer and a hypnotherapist. I do a lot of hypnotherapy audio programs for friends and families as well, and I have a lot of friends who are also doing hypnotherapy. What I found in the hypnotherapy world is people have become so conditioned to talking in a particular way, that anytime they're asked to speak or talk, or do a video, they go into this hypnotic voice that they have, and they start speaking like that. I'm thinking, why are you doing that? When I talk to you one-on-one you don't speak like that, so why are you speaking like that on camera?

If you're doing that, people will just switch off and it'll turn people off, and they'll instantly not watch your video because it's just boring. You don't want that to be you.

If you don't want to be a monotonous speaker, then put a heartbeat in your speech by varying your voice from Auditory to Visual to Kinaesthetic and back again, that is what we call the Charisma Pattern. Vary your tone throughout your presentation. Like I said, your normal-sounding voice is what you use 60% of the time, which I do clearly. Within that, there's got to be some kind of excitement and passion in your voice. There'll be instances where you raise the volume a little bit and bring that volume down as well to create that little impact for your audience. Remember to use your tonality and vary your voice by using your Auditory voice, your Warrior voice and your Kinaesthetic voice.

SUMMARY - Key Points to Remember About Tonality:

- The Charisma Pattern is starting with the Auditory voice tone, then move into the Visual voice and then into to the Kinaesthetic voice.
- The Auditory voice tone is medium pace, rhythmical and clear. If it was a sound wave, it would be a medium wave.
- The Visual voice tone is fast, loud and punchy. If it was a sound wave, it would be a short wave.
- The Kinaesthetic voice tone is slow, quiet, heartfelt, and breathy, with lots of pauses in between. If it was a sound wave, it would be long waves.
- Move your audience emotionally with your voice.
- Vary your tonality at least 20 – 40% of the time when you present.
- In order to master this, use numbers or the alphabet to practice varying your voice tonality.

CHAPTER 7
PUTTING IT ALTOGETHER

So there you have the complete guide to attaining outstanding presentation skills. These are the cutting-edge tools that true professional speakers are using. Now you have the same opportunity to master the same skills in this book, "Perform Like A Champion Every Time You Speak."

Here's a summary of all the core skills individually to act as a quick reference for you:

INTERESTING – Remember to always be yourself.

Key Points to Remember About Interesting:

- Embrace and accept your awkwardness, weirdness and strange mannerisms because this is what makes you unique and stand out from the rest.
- Determine what style and brand you are and demonstrate that as a speaker.
- Dress comfortably at all times whilst you are speaking or presenting.
- Express yourself honestly, truthfully and authentically.
- Always address the elephant in the room, as in, acknowledge whatever shows up during your presentation.

- Determine what your values are and what you stand for as an individual.
- Know your content and speak unconsciously so you can be more conversational whilst presenting.
- Take care of what you focus on, manage your breathing by pausing more and only use positive internal language towards yourself.
- Ultimately, know yourself, be yourself and be comfortable in your own skin while speaking or presenting to an audience.

MOVEMENT – Remember to always move with purpose.

Usage of the Warrior Gesture

The main use of the warrior gesture is to ultimately call your troops (audience/delegates) to take some form of action as a result of hearing you speak or present.

You use it to punch up your message by emphasising certain key words or phrases during your presentation.

You most definitely want to use the warrior gesture a lot towards the end of your presentation because it will help to call your army (audience/delegates) to action so they can act on your message.

Usage of the Lover Gesture

The main use of the lover archetype is to convey the message of openness and trust to your audience. You most definitely want to use this movement a lot at the beginning of your presentation. It helps to boost your relationship with the audience.

Another important fact to note here is, if you like to wear long-sleeved shirts whilst presenting, then you need to take off your cufflinks or unbutton your cuffs and fold up your sleeves to reveal your forearms. You see, if open palms represent being open and trustworthy then revealing your forearms represents even more trust. Many years ago we didn't shake hands; we actually used to shake forearms to check that the other person was not concealing any daggers. So, most often when you see me speak, I will have my sleeves rolled up to reveal my forearms for this very reason.

So there you have it; the lover sign illustrates that you are honest, authentic, genuine and a normal, regular person that can be trusted and believed.

Usage of the Sage Gesture

The main use of the sage archetype is to convey to your audience that you are an expert in the area in which you teach and that you really know your stuff.

It is also a very useful pose to be in when taking questions from your audience. It buys you time to think and consider the question before answering it. What do I mean? Well, as a speaker or presenter, get into the habit of repeating word for word any questions you are asked by your audience member. This will allow everyone to hear what the question was, as it might relate to them or be similar to what they wanted to ask. More importantly, it buys you valuable seconds of thinking time. The person who also asked the question feels appreciated as they feel you are taking your time to really consider the question before you answer it.

It is a great gesture to use when someone is sharing their story, a statement of fact or history that is related to a timeline. For instance, something that happened in the past, something that is happening in this present time or something that is going to happen in the future, e.g. *"25 years ago I came to the UK"; "What am I doing now? That is a great question, what I'm doing now is…"*; and finally, *"Did you know that in 2020 the world is going to change dramatically for the better? Let me elaborate…"* It's a great pose to have in those moments.

Usage of the Jester Gesture

It's very useful when you are telling a joke or saying something funny.

It's also great for telling stories that really captivate your audience. In storytelling it is the "Show & Tell" aspect of the story that really makes it come alive. Bring the audience into your world and allow them to relate to you on a deeper level. Express your emotions completely throughout the process of your story.

This gesture amplifies the comedian in you.

It's used to temper your own ego so you don't take yourself too seriously.

It makes you come across to your audience as someone who is entertaining and fun to be around.

It also allows you to let yourself off the hook and to be okay with not being Mr/Mrs Perfect. In other words, it's okay to make mistakes and not have all the answers.

Usage of the Sovereign Gesture

It is useful for making factual statements, things that are undeniably true. For example, *"This is the way it is… And it's not going to change for you or anyone!"* or *"Life is for living, and to live you have to give that which you seek to have, period."*

It allows you to assert your authority in a very calm and measured way without making you out to be a dictator or authoritarian.

It also allows you to emphasise certain words and punch them out in a calm and assured manner.

Usage of the Neutral Gesture

It makes you stand out from your fellow professional speakers, making you appear more professional, polished and grounded.

It makes it easy to transition between the other archetype movements like the warrior, lover, sage, jester and sovereign.

It's your central point where you start from and move out of into another gesture and move back to.

Key Points to Remember About Movement:

Don't overuse the same gesture.

Always go back to neutral when not in show and tell or gesturing.

Don't move all of the time; remember, pace, plant and present. Stillness is very powerful, especially when you are delivering your impact line, golden nugget, take away, keep phrase or foundational messages.

Use your characters' gestures, especially when telling a story.

Let your emotions drive you; show and tell 360 degrees.

Use bigger gestures for bigger audiences.

Have an animated face, meaning use your facial expressions whilst speaking or presenting to enhance or exaggerate the point you're making. It is worth practicing in front of the mirror using all your facial muscles.

Make smiling your main gesture and ensure you adopt it throughout your presentation if possible. This is especially important if you are speaking live to a camera or doing a live video recording.

The key to movement is, you have to move purpose and deliberately, otherwise don't move at all.

PRESENCE – Remember to always show up when you speak.

Key Points to Remember About Presence:

Presence is the difference that makes a difference.

The main factors that affect your state as a speaker are your physicality, the way you stand and your breathing patterns. Learn to find your rhythm as a speaker.

Show up 100%, not 99%. You are either present or not there at all. No half measures here.

Learn to pause more whilst speaking, as it will assist you on two counts. One, it will allow your audience to think and relate to what you are saying and secondly, it allows you time to gather your thoughts.

Remember, think fast and speak slowly so you find your own tempo and rhythm and maintain it.

Maintain an upright stance so you can use all of your available height whilst presenting.

Your energy is very important for being present. Remember, the energy you show up with is the energy your audience will pick up on.

Express yourself emotionally – meaning use your body and facial expressions to convey your message.

AWARENESS – Remember to always take in the whole picture.

Key Points to Remember About Awareness:

Manage your state so you can focus your attention on your audience's state.

Research various ways in which you can help change your audience's mood and state.

Utilise whatever shows up or happens in the room during your presentation to your advantage.

You need to expand your awareness beyond the individual to the whole room using the skills of peripheral vision or expanded awareness.

CONNECTION – Remember to always make your audience feel good.

Key Points to Remember About Connection:

Make smiling your standard gesture.

Select people in your audience to look at randomly.

Direct your eye contact from the front of the room, to the back of the room, to the left of the room and to the right of room.

Hold the audience member's gaze for about 15-20 seconds or more in some cases, at least until you finish your train of thought with that person. Then select a different audience member.

When you are speaking to a large audience of 5,000 – 10, 000, you will need to occasionally look at the camera straight ahead of you and speak directly to it. As the audience looks at you, they will feel that you are looking directly into their eyes, especially when you are presenting.

Make your audience feel special, unique and valuable by connecting with them individually during your presentation.

TONALITY – Remember to always use your full vocal range when speaking.

The Charisma Pattern starts with the Auditory voice tone, then move into the Visual voice then into to the Kinaesthetic voice.

The Auditory voice tone is medium pace, rhythmical and clear. If it was a sound wave, it would be a medium wave.
The Visual voice tone is fast, loud and punchy. If it was a sound wave, it would be a short wave.

The Kinaesthetic voice tone is slow, quiet, heartfelt and breathy, with lots of pauses in between. If it was a sound wave, it would be long waves.

Move your audience emotionally with your voice.

Vary your tonality at least 20 – 40% of the time when you present.

In order to master this, use numbers or the alphabet to practice varying your voice tonality.

TOSIN OGUNNUSI'S SPEAKING JOURNEY

As a child I was very talkative and playful, and one of my earliest memories was when my Dad's friends came over to the house for a game of draughts and beer.

My Dad would call me over and ask me to tell them a story. I was only 4 years old at the time, and I would be so excited because I knew there was a reward of Coca-Cola or Fanta at the end of it.

I would just start telling a story that was completely made up and I would have them in fits of laughter.

As the years went by, this natural talent and ability within an innocent child (me) was soon beaten out of me completely.

My home culture kicked in and Dad became very strict. You were seen but not heard, and we had this crazy rule called OBC (Obey Before Complaining), meaning if something happened and it wasn't your fault you were punished first and questions were asked later. And even when they discovered that you were innocent and not in the wrong, no one apologised to you. This was a regular occurrence in our household.

All this added to the stress of my father being very poor. Having to feed and take care of 16 children on one salary was very tough for him.

It meant that this innocent boy became very insecure and vulnerable. I felt inferior to others and I didn't believe in myself. I became very soft-spoken because I was always afraid to speak up, for fear I might get punished for saying the wrong thing or just speaking my mind. It was a very horrible feeling for me, and I lived with this fear for many years.

This fear also led me to stammer every time I found myself arguing with someone or speaking too fast, trying to defend myself. As I grew up people would look at me and say, he seems really confident, because I found it easy to meet people and connect with them. But the truth was I was an introvert who enjoyed his own company.

I grew up with no real role model in the family that I could look up to. As a matter of fact, most of my siblings looked up to me. Go figure (it was a case of the blind leading the blind). Lol!

I was fine as long as I was only dealing with people one to one. If I ever found myself in a group of people I was the quietest one in the group and only spoke when I was spoken to, because this was my conditioning growing up. We were told what to do, how to do it and when to speak and when to shut up. Some might say I'm over-dramatising the situation, but that's what it was really like. I hated it, especially the way it made me feel inside.

I yearned to be that 4-year-old again - totally free, expressing himself freely and making people laugh and happy, but he was buried deep inside me and I didn't know how to release him from my own self-created prison. It was as if someone had locked him up and threw away the keys.

Like I said, as the years went by and I grew up, I'd learnt to live with it. I'd accepted that this is who I was and there was no need or reason for changing.

This changed when my best friend was getting married and he made me his Best Man. The whole experience of the wedding preparations and the wedding itself was truly magical.

I was my playful self with the family and bridesmaids, organising the whole wedding and preparing the stag do. Everything was great and running smoothly, and then the day of the wedding came.

The church service was held at Our Lady of Delours in Hendon, and the wedding reception was at the Royal Banqueting Centre, which was in Finchley Central on Ballards Lane.

Three hundred people were invited to the reception.

I had written out my best man speech a month before the wedding and I'd been rehearsing it for weeks. I knew what to say, and I was feeling good about it until my name was called out to give the Best Man's speech.

As I stood up, I was struck dumb. My heart was pumping louder than usual. I was sweating profusely. I was so visibly nervous. This was the jovial guy who had made everyone laugh during the preparation stages, and everyone had this false perception of me being really confident, but I wasn't really.

I was standing there and 300 pairs of eyes were all on me, encouraging me to speak up. If this was a seminar and not a wedding, then there would have been some very angry delegates who would be walking out of the event and demanding their money back. But luckily for me, it was a wedding.

My mate looked at me and said, *"Come on, Tosin, you can do it!"* I knew the words, but as I opened my mouth nothing came out. I just simply froze. It was a very strange feeling, and as more people encouraged me to speak up it just made it worse.

I ran out to compose myself, feeling bad that I was ruining my best friend's wedding.

This was the worst experience of my life because it wasn't all about me. It was someone else's special day.

It was this experience that prompted me to seek mentors in this arena (speaking) so I could improve my presentation skills and public speaking skills.

I made a commitment to myself that I would never ever feel like this again.

So, that's where the journey began. The question you might be asking is, Tosin, what did you do? I'm glad you asked!

Firstly, I joined Toastmasters International, and within two years I became a "Competent Toastmaster". It was an interesting journey, and for my final speech I had to give a motivational speech.

Here is the full script of the speech that I gave:

CTM – COMPETENT TOASTMASTER SPEECH NUMBER 10

AN INSPIRATIONAL SPEECH BY TOSIN OGUNNUSI

TITLE: STEP OUT AND BE MORE OF WHAT YOU ALREADY ARE!!!

OUTCOME:

- To raise awareness of who we are as spiritual beings
- To inspire my audience to take massive action by stepping up to grab the opportunity to express their God-given gifts.

REASONS FOR SPEECH:

- To deliver the best speech I have ever delivered at a Toastmasters Club
- To complete my first Toastmasters manual and obtain my CTM (Competent Toastmasters Award)

INTRODUCTION:

Good evening Mr. President, chairman, toastmasters, fellow toastmasters and more importantly, our very welcome guest.

I bet at this stage, you are all wondering what sort of a statement that is, "Step Out and Be More of What You Already Are!" Let me ask you a question, how many of you in this room have dreamt of becoming a better public speaker?

Great! Now let me proceed to tell you something you may not be aware of. Whether you know it or not, everyone in this room right now is a professional speaker in their own unique way! Right now, some of you are wondering what planet is he from because that is definitely not me; that's okay, you may not believe it now but that's the truth about you. I know I certainly did not believe it until I joined this club.

A beautiful excerpt from James Allen's book, "As a Man Thinketh", will help to further clarify what I mean. Listen very carefully, because the dreamers are the builders. It states, "Dream lofty dreams, and as you dream, so you shall become. Your VISION is the promise of what you shall one day BE; your IDEAL is the prophecy of what you shall at last UNVEIL. The greatest achievement was at first, and for a time, a dream. The oak sleeps in the acorn; the bird waits in the egg; and in the highest vision of the soul, a waking angel stirs. Dreams are the seedlings of realities. Your circumstances may be uncongenial, but they shall not long remain so, if you but perceive an ideal and strive to reach it. You cannot travel WITHIN and stand still WITHOUT."

Now, you know that the true professional speaker lies within us all, because the truth about us is that we are spiritual beings encased in this limited and physical body, but spirit is always striving for full expression and expansion. And the more we hang on to our inhibitions, the unhappier we become. I am here today to recruit your souls and to encourage you all to step up and fully express your God-given gifts as speakers, because that's why you are here. Some of you might be sitting there saying it is easy for you, Tosin, because you know how to. I just want you to know I am no different from any of you, because when I walked through those doors two years ago, I was terrified of speaking in public.

This is my story:

All my life I have been very shy, reserved, very self-conscious, and had a lot of negative beliefs about myself, such as I stammer, I get overly anxious about everything, I don't have the right qualifications for speaking, and society taught me to believe that since I am black I would not be accepted. I mean, I was so bad I could not lead a silent prayer in front of a small group.

But every time I was by myself, I always wanted to be a motivational speaker to inspire others to live their dream. So deep inside of me, there was a strong desire to speak but I didn't know how. And whenever the opportunity came up, my limiting beliefs would stop me from expressing myself, hence I felt more unhappy and used to envy those that could speak very well in public. So, what has changed?

I went to a seminar where I met my first mentor Bob Proctor, who proceeded to explain how our mind works and why we do the things we do. After the seminar, I was buzzing with energy and enthusiasm. My whole being came alive because up until then I was kept captive by my old limiting beliefs and I didn't know how to get out mentally.

And for the first time, I got the opportunity to speak in public. I was so scared and nervous that I actually remember vividly wishing the ground would open so I could sink in and disappear. I was so shocked at the end of my talk that the other seminar participants came over to me and congratulated me on my talk. If they only knew how I felt inside, and I was still shaking inside not believing I had actually done it. It was at this seminar that Toastmasters International was mentioned to me.

Toastmasters International, and more importantly this club, Athenians, has been the difference for me. It created the right environment, the right blend of experiences, a fantastic mixture of cultures, or as Owen Murphy would put it – a mini UN! The guys here are warm, friendly and very supportive. That was encouraging for me and it really helped me to relax very quickly knowing that there were people here genuinely willing and able to help.

It wasn't easy looking back at the two years. I started off with my first speech:

1. THE ICE BREAKER – "A Little Boy's Wish", where I introduced myself to my fellow members.

2. SPEAK WITH SINCERITY – "An Introduction to The Power of The Mind", where I talked about how the mind worked. It was a topic I was very passionate about because it really explained why I was the way I was, and why I was doing things I didn't want to.

3. ORGANISE YOUR SPEECH – "Goals", where I talked about the purpose of a goal, how to set one and how to achieve it.

4. SHOW WHAT YOU MEAN – "The Terror Barrier", where I talked about what holds us back from taking the action we want in life.

5. VOCAL VARIETY – "I Will Win", where I acted out a poem. It was overly dramatic, but I lived it. It was something different.

6. WORKING WITH WORDS – "The Essence of Time in all Relationships", a funny speech as each time I said, *"It takes time in a relationship"* everybody responded by saying, *"Oh really, Tosin"*!

7. APPLY YOUR SKILLS – "Universal Law", which was prepared in 10 mins. The week before, I had just

run a workshop with a couple of other Toastmaster members on how to prepare a speech in 10 mins, and the following week I was put on the spot to practice what I preach, and I did not hesitate once. It felt like my best speech ever.

8. ADD IMPACT TO YOUR SPEECH – "Languages". I experimented with this speech. I proceeded to talk about learning a foreign language and then turned it around to talking about the language we would all love to learn about – the five love languages.

9. PERSUADE WITH POWER – "The Power of Choices", where I talked about the power of now and living in the moment by making current choices.

All of that has led me to today. So you see, the speaker you see before you today has always been inside of me since I was born, but I never allowed my spirit to fully expand and express itself the way I wanted due to my old conditioning.

This has been my greatest realisation and learning over the past two years.

The five main things that have helped me to develop as a speaker are as follows:

1. I made a decision – commitment, focus, consistency and discipline
2. I set goals for myself
3. I chose a few mentors to model myself on
4. I took massive action – action is the key ingredient!
5. I was not afraid to experiment and be creative

I want to encourage you all to make a decision today and to begin to expand and express your spirit. Let go of all your inhibitions and start to become that which you already are deep inside.

And as Nelson Mandela said:

"Our deepest fear is not that we are inadequate. Our deepest fear is that we are powerful beyond measure. It is our light, not our darkness, that most frightens us."

Well, ladies and gentlemen, I have just shared my light with you, in the hope it will help you to discover yours so you too can share it with others. Toastmasters.

It was an inspired speech, so if you are someone who's always had a longing to share your message with the world or someone who just has a desire to speak in public then know this: You're already a great speaker, you just need to realise it. Believe in yourself and dedicate yourself to learning the craft and it won't be long before the rest of the world sees you for who you really are.

The Toastmasters experience was great, but I found it a bit too rigid and formal. The way the teachings happen meant that you just wrote a speech, with a beginning, middle and ending and you memorised it and delivered it.

Something was fundamentally missing for me, and that was interacting with the audience. The rigid structure of the training didn't really allow for true engagement with the audience. Now I'm talking way back in 1999 and early 2000.

Things may have changed now, I'm not too sure as I'm not a part of Toastmasters International anymore. But it was a great start for me, and I would highly recommend it for anyone beginning their journey in public speaking. It also guarantees you an audience every week.

My research led me to Tampa, Florida, where I invested $20,000 plus flights and accommodation for 2 weeks to learn from one of the most charismatic, funny and extremely professional speakers and trainers, Topher Morrison.

It was here that I learnt how to really tell a story that can captivate the audience's imagination, how to conduct interviews, how to be an interviewee, how to address the media and deal with awkward questions, how to become a keynote speaker and how to conduct panel interviews, etc.

It was a real eye-opener, completely different from Toastmasters International.

Being better in terms of my stage performance meant that I could be a better trainer and truly engage every single participant at my events. Running empowerment activities also meant that I needed to help people feel good and safe to participate in activities that potentially could injure them. So having these skills for me and my business was simply priceless.

Now my training didn't stop there, as I'm always looking to improve myself and better my skills.

So, in 2009 I reconnected with my earlier mentor Andy Harrington by attending his 4-day Public Speakers University and in 2010 I became a life member of his Professional Speakers Academy. I spent time learning, growing and honing my skills.

I very quickly became one of his top trainers and was involved in all of his training sessions from one-day preview events to his seven-day Elite Speaker Training.

Here, I learnt how to be conversational with my message and how to structure my presentations so I didn't need notes, which meant I could be fully present and expressive with my audience. It was a game changer.

In June 2016, my services were no longer required and that's when I set up my own 3-day "Speaking & Presenting with IMPACT Training" teaching, "The F1 Speaker System." Later that year I was voted "The Professional Speakers Academy's Trainer of the Year 2016!"

My speaking career has seen me travel the world: the USA (New York, Florida), Australia (Melbourne, Sidney, Brisbane, Hamilton Island), Singapore, Malaysia, Romania, Kenya, Ukraine, Poland, the Czech Republic, and the UAE (Dubai, Abu Dhabi) just to mention a few.

Since then I have been constantly learning and growing from other professional speakers whilst teaching and mentoring my own clients to speak and present with IMPACT!

OTHER MENTORS THAT HAVE MADE AN IMPACT IN TOSIN'S SPEAKING CAREER:

BOB PROCTOR
Bob was Tosin Ogunnusi's first ever mentor where he got the licence to teach Bob's programmes (Born Rich and Goal Achievers).

TONY ROBBINS
Tony was Tosin's second mentor, and this is where Tosin's passion for empowerment activities was born. Tosin has attended Tony's flagship event UPW (Unleash the Power Within) 9 times: 5 times as a delegate and 4 times as a crew-member at UPW. This training, along with Tony's Mastery University, gave Tosin a real insight into how Tony teaches and conducts himself, and from a speaking point of view he learnt a lot about how to tell stories and really engage your audience.

LES BROWN
Les has always been a personal mentor of Tosin. Tosin loves his ability to tell stories and really engage his audiences. Tosin has attended his events in London and regularly watches and listens to a lot of his videos and audio programs.

AMYN DAHYA
Amyn is the mentor who has really grounded Tosin. Amyn is Tosin's spiritual mentor, but to Tosin he's more than that – more like a father figure. Amyn taught Tosin how to meditate and Tosin has been meditating regularly for close to 20 years now.

This puts Tosin in a very unique position where he has the ability to hold his audience's attention with his energy and temperament. He is a great listener and an outstanding speaker all rolled into one.

TESTIMONIALS

From an early age and following in the footsteps of my mum and dad, I've always been an avid reader, a devourer of knowledge. My favourite word was, and continues to be, "Why?" as my inquisitive mind seeks to find reasons behind life's many wonders and challenges!

Meeting Tosin in February 2019 and being introduced to his book "Time to break free" have been life-changing! Now my equally favourite word is "How?" "How can I become a skilled speaker and presenter like Tosin?" "How can I motivate others in their personal and professional careers?" "How can I deliver presentations that inspire, demystify, delight?

At school I loved drama (often the leading lady!) and was always the first to volunteer to read at school assembly. "How could I channel these passions in my business life?" I was incredibly fortunate to meet Tosin at a time when I felt I was at the crossroads of choosing between a life that didn't hold much excitement and one which held much promise. One coaching session on how to structure and deliver a presentation was all it took for the 'curtain' to rise.

Becoming a presenter myself and delivering inspirational stories has now become, with Tosin's support, a realistic goal. So now Tosin's sequel 'Perform like a champion...' is a welcome and timely publication. By breaking down the elements of public speaking into bite-sized chunks, I love the fact that you can pick it up, put it down, re-read, practice, double-check that your performance as a speaker is 'on track'. Sometimes, the smallest detail makes the biggest effect - a pause, a gesture, a facial expression - and Tosin's book 'How to have outstanding presentation skills' is a must-read if you wish to deliver presentations that engage, thrill, and captivate your audience. Thank you Tosin for all your support, feedback and encouragement. And congratulations on your latest 'How to book!

~Heather Hilder-Darling - BA(Hons) FIDM MARLA, Callaways Limited. Land & Brand New Homes Limited

Tosin is warm, switched on, energetic, giving & thankful. Having been taught by Tosin, I can say, not only is he an expert speaker but a true role model in every sense of the word & I'm thankful to be his student.

~James Scollard - Property Expert

A great insightful read that is well presented in a thoughtful manner of key practical steps for success for the reader. The book is written in an engaging and authentic way that captivates your attention. Well done Tosin - great job.

~Linda Attram - Founder – Mothers in Business

The 1973 R.H.Brusking Associate's study published in London Sunday Times, that the no.1 fear for most people is public speaking, even before death which was ranked no. 7. And still to this day. Tosin is reminding us in his latest book, we speak in public every day! It is an innate skill we all possess - we just need to step up and be ourselves.

Beautifully structured and enriched with useful tips, Tosin's "Perform Like A Champion Every Time You Speak" is the best companion to give you public speaking confidence and transform the way you approach presentations or trainings.

As a marketing person I am often asked to deliver presentations or to speak at different events - Tosin's teachings really helped me overcome my public speaking anxieties and negative emotions associated with it, by using them to my advantage rather than my disadvantage.

Practice makes perfect! So I am very glad that he decided to publish his teachings and make them available in a handy format such as this book!

~Gabriela Galatanu - Marketing Director, Romania

Tosin's book is a golden nugget for any professional who speaks in front of an audience. It's very well structured and it delivers a ton of techniques that you can use right away in your presentations. But above all, Tosin teaches you how to think like a leader, how to install success mindsets that will really help you to influence your public.

Each chapter ends with key points, so after you read the whole book you can return and simply implement the essentials that you've learnt when you have to prepare a speech. It's a book that I will use over and over again in my presentations.

~Dragos Stoian - Trainer, Speaker and Founder of Public Speakers League Romania

Tosin is genuinely passionate about public speaking and he has collated his ideas and teachings into this brilliant book. He has a unique ability to help people overcome their fear of public speaking and has motivated so many individuals from diverse backgrounds to achieve their goals. He uses his skills to connect and communicate to make a really powerful impact so that anyone that has a passion for public speaking can use the cutting-edge tools featured in this book.

~Anita Goyal - Philanthropist and Author

This book is just great! I had many books on public speaking in my hands. This one definitely stands out with the amount of specific, practical knowledge that Tosin is fully committed to sharing with examples. You can feel that the author really believes with great conviction that you the reader, you are able to become an exceptional speaker and he encourages you to do so in the book.

The book is written in a simple, accessible language, a lot of practical, detailed knowledge and the passion with which the author writes makes it a truly unique textbook for public speaking. A valuable book for both amateurs and professionals.

~Joanna Piec-Gajewska – Poland

Tosin's latest book is a revelation. I've attended several conferences where Tosin has presented and his ability to hold and lead the audience made me question how effective I am presenting to others as he's on another level. What I found from reading 'Perform Like a Champion Every Time You Speak' was that there's no magic at play. Just an ordered system which Tosin breaks down and makes simple for anyone to use. His hidden code was particularly riveting – showing his mastery in understanding a knowledge. Anyone, seasoned or novice, can get loads of insight into presenting by reading this book and I would encourage all presenters to do so!

~*John Penquet – Managing Director, Light Lettings Ltd.*

Most books on speaking are about how to create captivating content. Tosin goes beyond that, as even the most amazing content will be lost if you do not grab the attention of your audience by mesmerizing them with HOW you speak. Tosin gives you the tools to know how to master the stage by the way you move, you speak and you connect with your audience. He shows you all the tricks that will make you unforgettable for your audience.

~*Denisa Říha Palečková - Expert on Love and Intimacy*

I really looked forward to reading this book from Tosin as I had awesome training from him to enable me to be a speaker at an event and tell my story. This book is well thought out and is easy to follow. The walk through format of the book makes it easy to structure your talk and how you want it to run. I really like the photos as it explains the use of stances and poses, as they say a picture is worth a thousand words.

In short, if you want to learn how to deliver your story or any content with poise and confidence then this is the book for you!

~Barrie McDowell – Director at Luscombe & Co.

This is a fantastic book with excellent advice and cutting edge tools for anyone wanting to improve their presentation skills. Brilliantly articulated throughout with a clear, easy to follow framework that will help you no matter what stage you are in your public speaking journey. Tosin is clearly a master at his game. Look no further, this book is a must read for anyone who aspires to share their message with the world!

~Nasim Patel – CEO/Managing Director, Go Haven

Tosin is one of the best performers I've ever seen. He is dynamic, funny, fascinating and most importantly, he is completely authentic. This authenticity makes him worth to follow, especially if you want to learn the tricks of becoming an excellent performer.

~Eszter Komonday - Coach, Supervisor, AUDI Hungary

Having attended a 3 day Speaking with Impact course presented by Tosin Ogunnusi I couldn't wait to read his latest book, 'Perform Like A Champion Every Time You Speak'. I am not a natural speaker and the thought of speaking in front of an audience terrified me, questions like, what if I forget what to say, what if I am boring? All these negative thoughts would be running through my mind. I wanted to be a better public speaker so I could become the face of my business and build trust with potential clients. Tosin is an exceptional speaker and highly motivating in assisting me in breaking down my personal barriers and changing my mindset. By following Tosin's simple steps, on the course and within the book, I was able to challenge my fears and overcome them and present on a number of occasions to different audiences. The book re-enforces the principles I learned on the course and is a great source of reference to keep my development on track. This has directly affected my business as I am now seen as an expert in my field. I cannot recommend the book highly enough.

~Helen Pass BSc (Hons) – Director, HomeSmart Lettings

Tosin has a truly unique gift, or rather a mission that he accomplishes step by step in his life. That is enabling other people to fly – dream big and make their dreams become reality. He helps them lose their fears and overcome whichever obstacles in their way. His new book 'Perform Like A Champion Every Time You Speak', in which he focuses on the improvement of public speaking skills, is another step forward. No matter the size of your audience, or what your goal is, I believe that Tosin's encouraging guidance can enhance your performance in many areas of your everyday life.

~Michaela Dlouha - Teacher of Czech and Creative Writing, Poet, Journalist, Founder of Tallinn Creative Writers

Tosin's energy and passion for his work is boundless. He deserves every success he creates for himself through his hard hard-work and commitment.

~Karyn Pritchard – Business Coach

Tosin continues to inspire, over the two decades that I have known him, he has always been at the forefront of Personal Development. And this book doesn't disappoint, Tosin shares a plethora of tools and techniques that when embraced are guaranteed to transform your life.

~Caroline Shola Arewa - Coach, international Speaker and Best Selling Author of Opening to Spirit

Tosin has managed to pack the commonly known and also hidden secrets to public speaking that only a few of us use consistently, into a great guide for potential public speakers. A useful toolbox of ideas that as I read it could hear Tosin's powerful voice of passion coming through. A great guide for people wanting to start or polish their public speaking skills.

~Steve Consalvez - The world's #1 Firewalking Instructor Trainer

Coming from somebody who has severe stage fright, everything Tosin taught me has been life changing. Putting the advice from this book into action will change everything for you, I can now present to audiences confidently which is a necessity for me at work, I even enjoyed the last time I was on stage and got great feedback! All because of the presentation skills I took from Tosin, it is possible for anyone!

~Nadine Willis - Area Manager, CGT Lettings

Learning to speak on stage is by far one of the biggest gifts you will give to yourself and the world. I discovered my speaking voice in 1996 and it has opened magical doors and opportunities beyond imagination.

A journey filled with fun, freedom, travel and the transformation of millions of people. I met Tosin at an event I had organised in 2005 and we quickly became very close friends. He took to personal development like a duck to water and his passion to make a difference has taken him on his own journey.

Today I stand proud of his work and journey so far, looking keenly to the future. One thing is for sure, reading this book will take you on your own journey and help you step into your power. Enjoy it!

~Kalpesh Patel - The Enlightened Entrepreneur and Co-Founder of www.WorldTransformationOrg.com

This book 'Perform Like A Champion Every Time You Speak' is a fantastic and well written book, compact and to the point!

When you follow the advices, use the tools, tactics and strategies you'll be amazed by the impact you'll have on your audience.

Tosin teaches you to deliver phenomenal results in a very easy and practical manner. He taught me the same way, and I am very grateful for that today. This book is a great guide and backup for me. An absolute must read for anyone who wants to Perform Like A Champion Every Time They Speak!

~Nelleke Scholten - The Unique Life Creator^{TM}

I have both worked in the personal development industry and now as a preacher. I can honestly say that Tosin is someone I have known for many years and I have always been impressed by the way he impacts an audience of any size with his charismatic way of presenting and high energy. Tosin is authentic and a mentor that any aspiring speaker should be looking to. Having read through this book, Tosin leaves nothing behind as he shares within the pages the steps needed to become a world class speaker and the techniques that many people today spend thousands of pounds to learn.

~Edward Lane – Entrepreneur and Preacher

Tosin, is a very experienced inspirational speaker, buy learning the skills he has set out in this great book, you too can share your story with the world confidently from stage.

~Mike Woods – Mike is the Author of the Amazon Best Selling Book, "How to SUCCESSFULLY Invest in Property" and Founder of Property Expert Partnership

Perform like a Champion is an outstanding book and a must-read for anyone serious to take their speaking career to the next level. Tosin is a brilliant story-teller and the book is very easy-to-read, well written and structured. It's one of those books that you can read over and over again and still find nuggets of wisdom and useful tips to help you progress your speaking skills. I don't think there's anyone who wouldn't benefit from reading this book.

~Irina Alionte - Irina Alionte founder of Bodyshape Transformation Romania

For anyone who is interested in public speaking and lacks the confidence or belief in themselves to do it successfully (like I use to be), then you need to read this book!

Tosin's power of delivery is just breathtakingly awesome. He is fantastic at teaching and is able to put things in a way that you can then relate to which makes the whole learning process a lot easier and certainly more enjoyable. I'm sure that there are many Speaker coaches out there and perhaps you have listened to some of them but I myself would look no further than Tosin for my own personal development coaching.

In less than a year, Tosin has coached me to speak in public with confidence and belief and I put myself to the test at a conference in a room full of 300 people in October this year which I delivered to perfection (even if I do say so myself). Buy this book! It will change your life!

~Vittorio Fierro – Managing Director, City and County (Peterborough's Leading Independent Estate Agent established in Peterborough since 1980)

Over the last year, I have been lucky enough to be coached by Tosin on public speaking and it's only down to his training that I now have the confidence to present at events of several hundred people.

This book is all of Tosin's valuable coaching written down, from the advice on stance, to being aware of your tonality, right through to, how to craft your story. His training is engaging, easy to follow and really unlocks your potential as a speaker. If you follow his carefully crafted advice in this book, you'll feel comfortable speaking in front of groups of people in no time.

~Angharad Truman - CEO CGT Lettings

I love this book - having known Tosin for 7 years now I love the honesty of his past (I didn't know this before) and how this led him to be one of the best public speakers I have ever had the pleasure to meet and work with, Tosin has used his 25+ years of experience in the industry to help and support people wanting to be better in this field - I have a large team all over the world in Network marketing and their biggest fear is public speaking so I know this book will really help them. Thanks Tosin.

~Debbie Nwangwa - Soaring manager, Forever living products UK

Thank you for always thinking of and including me each time you write a book. Your books have always left me feeling that much more equipped and inspired.

This particular book I loved because they are areas I can completely resonate with. i.e. when you described your childhood and being naturally able to do storytelling and speak, then later finding that skill gone and being frustrated and confused about it later in adulthood. I love how you described unlocking that. This for me, as a reader, I took it as a skill I can transfer to various areas of my life and personal growth.

The book is also very specific on how to actually deliver or act, a good handbook for quick reference if preparing for, meeting, speaking etc.

Thank you for a fantastic, practical, inspirational and easy to read book.

~Ellen Sena – Entrepreneur, Healthcare UK, CEO/Trustee, Hear to Aid Foundation

If you apply even one thing from this book it will make you a better speaker, trainer and presenter. Apply more than one and you're onto a winner!

With clear explanations, instructions, images and reasons behind things the information in this book will help you understand and deliver your message more effectively.

It's easy to read and easy to implement, all you have to do now is just follow the instructions and get your message out into the world!

~Elizabeth Mansfield - Health, Wellness and Mindshift Coach

Having seen Tosin in action at our DVG STAR events I can definitely say that he has a unique flare in front of the audience. Especially the way he presents his speeches, he always never fails to attract the attention of the audience.

In this book 'Perform Like A Champion Every Time You Speak', Tosin has cleverly put together everything that you need to know to present an unforgettable speech. He has collated all the information into an easy to follow guide, making it compact and to the point!

By following his advice you will be sure to make an ever lasting impact on your audience. A highly recommended book for anyone wanting to become a speaker.

~Labosshy Mayooran - Clinical Scientist, Managing Director & Co-Founder of DVG STAR and an Award –Winning Author

Mastering public speaking is a very important skill to learn. Tosin has helped me improve my public speaking skills and I know this book will help others do the same.

~Avnish Goyal - Chairman Hallmark Care Homes

Tosin is one of the most inspiring people I know of. I met him for the first time few years ago on the public speaking academy training and since the first moment I have noticed amazing passion, energy and wisdom that he would inspire myself. As a bodyworker, holistic healer and entrepreneur I found Tosin's message to be extremely useful. Tosin also helped me to improve my business and expand on my public speaking skills so that I can reach thousands of people with my unique message. Thank you Tosin for sharing your joy and enthusiasm with us. You are amazing being. Namaste.

~Nisarga Eryk Dobosz - Founder at Integral Body Institute

Tosin himself embodies an infectious and exuberance of positive energy, both in life and through the pages of his books, and this one is no exception! He is a true master at not only his own presentations in front of a variety of audiences but being able to instil these skills to others, enabling them to challenge and overcome their fears and achieve their own personal best.

~Kate Gregory - Training, Events & Development Manager at Agent Rainmaker

Printed in Poland
by Amazon Fulfillment
Poland Sp. z o.o., Wrocław